Foreword
#1 Interna

ISABELL: THEN & NOW

The Life Behind the Movie "Say Something"

By: Isabell Rodríguez
Award Winning Actress and Author

LOCALEXPERTSGROUP

Local Experts Group
1111 Finch Ave West #401
Toronto Ontario Canada M3J 2V5
416.991.8131
www.LocalExpertsGroup.com

LocalExperts™
People Building Our Community

1st Printing
Printed in Canada

ISBN: 978-1-9995358-7-2

Table of Contents

Foreword

It is October 2018 and I am in London, United Kingdom, in Kensington for the very first time. I traveled from Canada to London because I was nominated for a Global Author's Award. This is where I first met Isabell Rodríguez, who was also at the Global Author's Awards. She had travelled from Sweden to the United Kingdom with her friend from the Global Woman Summit. After we finished speaking on stage, autographing books and networking, a group of non-Londoners went out for dinner. I found myself sitting next to Isabell who did not say a word for hours while we were eating dinner.

Finally, when everybody was quiet, I turned to Isabell and said, "So, Isabell, tell me about you?" She replied, "I am not an author yet, but I really want to be an author." I asked her, "What kind of books do you want to write?" She casually said, "I want to tell my story." Because I am an author and a book publisher, I jumped into talking about my principles I use to teach people about their books and in what order they should write them. I said, "You should write your story last. I teach about the 4 most important kinds of books to write, the ABCD books. A = Anthology, B = Business, C = Celebrity and D = Desire."

During the course of my conversation about the ABCD books, I realized Isabell was the only one not drinking. I remarked on the fact, and she told me she did not drink anymore. I was respectful of her choices for herself, but I was curious, so I asked why and she gave me a brief overview of what you are about to find out in the pages of this book.

This was interesting, but then Isabell mentioned something else to me, which was about the documentary. She said, "My story was so bad, that I was featured in a documentary," and I am like, "Documentary? Really? Tell me more."

Her documentary, "Say Something" was so popular that more than a million people have already seen it in Scandinavia. Now, she really had my attention, and I told her, "Oh, my ABCD book teaching does not apply to you because you are already a celebrity."

Isabell was very shy and she said, "I do not think so. I was young, and the film crew followed me around for about 5 years. The documentary was just to bring awareness to children growing up in domestic violence. It is to highlight the need for support and treatment."

I asked if there was more and learned this documentary had also won a prestigious award in Sweden. In 2017, "Say Something" won the Kristallen (the official Swedish television Award) for Best documentary of the year.

I was impressed and told Isabell to let me know if she needs any help, as I am both an author and a publisher.

Nothing happened while we were in London. We left to return to Canada and Sweden and went our separate ways. We connected later on Facebook. One day, she reaches out to me, "Raymond, I really want to do this, but I am not sure if I am ready."

We had a discovery phone call to see if this is the right time for Isabell and her story. I then discovered Isabell had been asked to give recommendations to the Swedish government on a legislative change to the laws governing domestic violence. A change that would see laws to criminalize the act of domestic violence in the presence of children come into being.

"Isabell, your story needs to be told; you need to write a book. Most people write a book to get credibility and visibility; you already have it. Do you have any idea how many people you could help?"

"You have a life-changing and a life-saving story that needs to be told."

"This is a topic I am very passionate about and I am super excited to work with you. I would be honored to publish your book."

Isabell responded, "I want to do this with my own money." I was impressed with her character because of this. After getting to know Hector, her husband, I knew he was doing really well in his business, so money was not an issue, but I understood Isabell's need for independence to tell her story.

It is a story many young children around the world go through, but many of them do not come back from the terror; they remain in the darkness.

A few months later, Isabell rang me up; she had her money to pay for her story to be published. And if that was not blessing enough, I now have a connection with her husband, Hector. So, not only am I publishing Isabell, but I am also coauthoring with Hector.

This all started because Isabell said "something" at our dinner in London. It is now your turn to, "say something"; it can only get better from here.

God Bless.,
World Civility Ambassador,
Dr. Raymond Harlall, Doctorate of Humanities (h.c.)
Publisher

Who Is Isabell Rodríguez?

For many years I ran away—mostly from myself. I could not handle everything I was feeling. I tried to cover it all up with poison substitutes. I thought I was a broken human being. However, it finally came to a point, when after being on the run for a while, I had no other choice, but to change.

I realized I was never broken; I just had not healed from the traumas I went through while growing up as a child. I needed to step out and see the whole picture. I needed to change my habits and choose another way of living, because the life I was living was sooner or later going to kill me.

Throughout my personal journey, I felt very lonely. I wished someone would have handed me a book or a course, anything in fact, so, I would know I was not alone and I could get out of it, even if it would take a lot of work.

If you identify yourself with any of that, or if you feel the same, then this book is for you.

I wrote this book because I know there are people like you who are feeling the same pain I felt. Or maybe, those days are in your past, but you are still struggling to move forward.

I want you to know you are not alone. And most of all, you can get out of it and become what you are meant to be.

If you feel like giving up or you are struggling to get back up, then allow me to help you with my story. If you know anybody who walks in those lonely shoes, this book is also for them to be inspired and to find strength, even in the darkest moments.

Today, I am a survivor of sexual abuse and violence. I am a coach, a speaker, and a blogger. I am happily married and have traveled to over 50 countries. I have found my place in the world... and I am here to help you find yours.

In 2017, my life movie "Say Something" was critically acclaimed and awarded with the "Kristallen Award" for best documentary.

In 2019, I was nominated for the "Aspirational Award" for the Global Women Club Awards.

"To know more about my journey, please visit my blog at www.issyrodriguez.com, where I share my experience, ideas and my advice. If you want me to help you personally, join me on my next workshop, where we will go through your story together and I will help you unlock the best version of yourself. To know more about the "Rebuild Your Life" program and workshop, go to www.rebuildyourlifeprogram.com.

Thank You

I have to start by thanking my amazing husband, Hector Rodríguez for always believing in me and pushing me to keep going, no matter what. To get this book done was also important for him, so thank you lovie.

To my beautiful mother, who went through the darkest times with me and who always stood by my side, even at my worst. She always believed in me. For all those times you brag about how much I have accomplished, thank you Mami.

To my brother, who is the biggest fighter I have ever met. You are my best friend. Thank you for giving me the best little human in this world, Michelle, my little niece. Thank you for always standing by my side no matter what. I love you Tjock-kurre.

To Mamos och babas, who always took care of me growing up and for keeping the memory of my father alive. A special thank you to Mamos who always showed me what a strong, patient woman looked like.

To Pillan, my best friend, for always pushing me forward, for always believing in me, and for all the crazy adventures you got me into.

A special thank you to the team of "Film and Tell" who made the "Say Something" documentary possible.

To Rebecka, my soul sister-friend, who brought spirituality to my life. You showed me what healing and the universe can do for your spirit and soul. Thank you for being an amazing friend, who always believed in me. Thank you so much.

To Raymond Harlall and his team for making this book a reality for me. Thank you, Raymond for helping me with the small and big details, for guiding me, and for pushing me to get this book done. I am super grateful.

Thank you to my coach and friend Sandra Wigren, who showed me the way, many times. You always saw the good in me. Thank you for being such an inspiring mentor in my life.

To Katarina Hansen, who opened up my vision and helped me so I could fight my inner saboteur. You are a kickass woman. I will always be super grateful for what you taught me.

A big thank you to the Global Woman Club and community for opening up so many doors, and being a platform for so many inspiring women, all around the world.

To my best cousin, Kim Westerlund, who keeps inspiring me every day and has always been by my side, no matter what. Thank you for being there for me at all times, making me feel strong and invincible. You are the best.

Tusen tack (thousands of thank-yous) to all of my friends I met in Norway. A special thank you to the people at Gardermoen Airport, for making my days better while working my ass off back in the days.

Thank you to my beloved family, Andersson for all the love you have always given me. Thank you, Matte for being the fighter you are and for helping us throughout the years. The same to Janne who always made me laugh.

Thank you, family, Ericsson. Thank you to all of my family on my father's side. You kept the memory of my father alive.

Thank you, Sebastian, my cousin who has always brought joy to my life, and for being there at my worst.

Thank you, Anne Järnberg, for being an extra mom to me. Thank you for helping my mom and me during our crisis. You are so important for many people. You are a great inspiration. You always keep a positive mindset no matter what.

Introduction

I thought writing about what happened years ago would be easy. I mean it happened years ago, but little did I know. I knew the story by heart, but putting it on paper and not just speaking it, was much harder. It was difficult to write my story, my truth, from my own perspective. There were many things I do not remember today, but with help from my old diaries, I was able to put it all together. This experience helped me to understand myself more—why I made certain decisions throughout my journey, why I reacted the way I always have, or why I had to be as low as I was, to be able to rise and pick myself up.

I wanted to write this book, so I could get my message out. Opening up and speaking is the best therapy, not only for yourself, but for others, as well. Something I felt my whole life, was nothing, but loneliness, emptiness of bittersweet escapes, self-hate and at times, extreme insecurity. Today, I know I was not born that way. It was my traumas, which carved me into that person. So, I became the person who reshaped myself into what I am today.

I rebuilt myself. It was a long journey and even today, I am still learning new ways to see life differently. If you put the twenty-year-old Isabell next to the woman, I am today they would be the same, but with a completely different vision, mindset and beliefs. The story is still there, but the past is no longer my burden. I am no longer a victim of my past. I built myself up after years of tearing myself down.

Every person has a story, and by telling yours, it can help others, which is the reason why I am writing my story. If one person can read this and get the tools to rebuild themselves and feel less alone, then my story was not for nothing.

For many years, I felt like I had so much inside of me I wanted to share. I thought, why not write a book about my experience. I was abused as a child. For many years, I thought something was wrong with me. I even received a bipolar diagnosis, which at first, seemed to be the right fit. But when I looked closer, I realized it was just a label they put on me. The real issue was my traumas. I never really "healed" myself from them, confronted them or even accepted them. I only thought whatever happened to me was years ago. It was in the past, and it cannot hurt me anymore, so I just let it go.

But in fact, it still lived inside of me, in many ways. My life started to take bad turns, because I could not handle all the pain and emotions, I had built up inside me. I needed to speak about it and not to run from it, which I did for many years. I hid it with drugs and alcohol. I used travel as an escape from reality. Every time I came back home, I felt worse and wanted to leave again. I wanted to run away from myself, which was impossible. I had to decide this was not how I wanted to live my life anymore. I needed to change.

I did not know how to change. I just needed to start. Starting was the hardest. Where should I begin? I believed I was completely broken, and nothing or no one could save me. I believed there was too much that needed to be fixed.

What I did not know back then was I was never broken. In fact, no one really is. We are just humans with flaws and a bag full of mistakes, but we are never broken. We do not need to be fixed by anything or anyone, just truly loved by our self, which for me was the hardest part. To love myself.

I had been insecure for as long as I could remember. My confidence was high, but my self-esteem was totally not there. I was super insecure. Self-esteem and self-confidence are two completely different things. Self-esteem refers to how you feel about yourself overall—how much esteem, positive regard or self-love you have. Self-esteem develops from experiences and situations, which have shaped how you view yourself today. To be self-confident is to trust in oneself, and in particular, in one's ability or aptitude to engage successfully or at least adequately with the world.

I compared myself to everyone and thought I would never be good enough in anything. I not only had bad thoughts about myself, but also had them about others. To make myself feel better, I found anything bad about another person. While growing up, I was envious of pretty and successful people, because I thought they were really lucky. This kind of thinking made me very down, more than just by being a jealous and insecure person. It was more like a hamster wheel in the wrong direction, bringing me further and further down.

Today, I see through another perspective. I am no longer insecure about myself or my self-worth. I have worked incredibly hard to get here. It was the small steps I took every day that put me on the right path. Little by little, I became what I always wanted to be. I met people on the way helping and pushing me, but I also met people who dragged me down and absolutely fooled me to believe they were my friends. But you learn along the way, this is what life is all about. Discovering the path for you and who you really are. What would that path be without those lessons? Would you even be half as strong, if you had not gone through it?

The truth is no one has it all figured out and everyone has a story. Some have a tough road, and some have a different one. Whatever road we have to walk, we can share it, so the next person or the people who are on the road right now, will feel less alone and get the advice they need at that moment in time.

With Much Love,
Isabell Rodríguez

CHAPTER I:

Stolen Innocence

My story started way back when I was fourteen months old, when my father suddenly died in a car accident. Growing up not having a father figure left a black hole that no one or anything could ever fill.

I wondered how life would have turned out if he would have been there or who I would have become. Not having my father also caused an immense inner stress because I was terrified of losing the only parent I had left, my mother. I started to have anxiety at a very early age; in fact, as long as I can remember.

I know today, not only did my father's death affect me in many ways, but it also affected everyone around me. Even though I was very little when he passed away, so much was left for me to think about. Who was this man, who did he want me to become, were we alike, etc.?

My mom took my dad's death very hard. She was left alone with two kids, my big brother, who is six years older than me and myself. We do not share the same father, but we grew up together and are super close. My mother struggled a lot while we were growing up to keep the money going all month long. She tried to do the very best she could.

Even when my father passed away, she tried to hold the family together at all costs. I know my mom did everything in her power to do the right thing and to love us the best that she could. But the truth is, my mother had a difficult past. My father's death did not make it easier for her. She searched desperately for love from different places.

My mom's first "boyfriend" as I can remember, came into our lives when I was around three years old. He had two children, a girl and a boy. This is when my second trauma started to take place. It started when I was three years old and lasted until I was around five years old. I was raped and used sexually by my step-brother, who was ten years old at the time. I only remember small parts of it, but it was big enough to take away the biggest thing in my life: my innocence as a child.

I was not aware of his games, as he called it. How would a three-year old girl know that putting a boy's penis in her mouth was wrong? My mom found out when I was sitting in the back of the car showing her on an ice-cream how I would play with his private parts, saying it was a game he had taught me to play. This caused many things for me and my family. How could you get a child to heal from this? My mother made the right choice to leave the man she was with, to take care of the whole situation and me. She looked for all the help she could get for me to overcome this trauma. But it was hard, because I was so young.

As I grew older, all the scars that my experience left started to show their marks more and more. I felt like an outcast. I was having big troubles handling my emotions, which was also one of my mother's big issues, as well. I would go from happy to an outburst in three seconds flat.

Not knowing why sometimes or how to stop it. Because of this, I was in trouble a lot in school.

I was different; I had trouble sitting still, listening and getting along with the other kids. I know today I needed more attention because when I was a young innocent girl, somebody stole my innocence from me by making me do things no child should ever experience. Because I was sexually abused, and it was not correctly dealt with, I suffered even more growing up, because nobody really addressed my behavior, which stemmed from what I had experienced.

I remember one special incident in school when I was in second grade. We had a class where we would practice the things we were not good at. I had to practice the alphabet, but what I really wanted to practice was handwriting. So, instead of sitting in my chair rambling the alphabets, I went over to the crayon board and started to write with a brush dipped in water, on the big gray board, next to some of my classmates.

They knew I was not supposed to be there; I knew it too. I just wanted to practice the same thing as they were doing. My classmates wanted to prove a point to me and they switched my water can to an empty can, so I could no longer practice my handwriting. First, I was upset and pretended I did not care, which I did, while they were laughing at me. But because of their laughs, I could not handle the feelings anymore, so I ran into the bathroom in the classroom to let myself cry in silence. A sadness that turned into a hysterical cry.

Minutes later, my teacher was knocking on the door, convincing me to let her in. When I did, she was angry. She did not seem to care why I was sad, nor was she trying to calm me down. Instead, she pushed me to the wall, strangling my throat, telling me to stop. Outside, I could hear my classmates. One of them opened the door, which my teacher had forgotten to lock. She immediately let go of my throat. Then, she started stroking my chin with her hand, trying to calm me down and dry my tears. She had switched in a second, almost like she was two different people. I remember feeling confused and weird about the whole situation.

Why would an adult do that? I remember thinking I was the problem. I was probably this annoying kid who she just had enough of. I kept coming up with so many excuses, because it was easier than to just admit she was wrong. No matter what issues she had with me, she handled it wrong and that is it. This is how I thought most of my life. Thinking I was wrong, no matter what, and caring too much about why other people did not like me. It was my fault and maybe I deserved it.

But to learn how to separate your own experience from your own actions, is super important. It was very clear as I became older, I needed to take responsibility for what I have been through and to take responsibility for my own actions. Not behaving badly just because I went through difficult things by myself when I was growing up. I never wanted to blame my past for misbehaving in school. I was just misunderstood while growing up. I was insecure, and I would have needed a strong person to lead the way.

I had a lot of anger, and to be able to handle the anger, I needed extra attention in school. I had an extra teacher who would sit with me when times became rough. I had piano lessons with her when I had too much energy, as I would not sit still in the classroom. We had a secret sign, so she would know when I needed a break. I also had a diary I would write in almost every day. I wrote to my Dad in the diary, to help me overcome my sadness about his death. It became my own healing book.

Because I was crying and acting out my emotions and missing my dad, I used the book to write messages to him. I would get it out on paper how much I missed him. She really was a super nice teacher with really good ideas to help me to get over my father's death. She saw the real me and not the "annoying kid" I was from the outside. She saw me as a wounded child who needed extra attention. She was only there for a while until she found another opportunity to teach music. I remember feeling so lost and lonely when she left. Now I had nobody to turn to when times became rough.

CHAPTER II:
A War Behind Closed Doors

Growing up, I only had my mom. She was my safety zone. She had three jobs from the time I was seven until I was eleven years old. She needed to work extra shifts to keep the food on our table. Often, I would only see her late at night. I needed to grow up fast and to handle things like cleaning and making my own food at an early age. This taught me how to be responsible, which was a positive thing for me. I remember missing her a lot, but she did the best she could, even if I needed her time more than I got it.

Because of my anxiety at an early age, I had some problems both in school and at home. I was always anxious about everything. I started to develop a hypochondrium, which one summer became really bad. I was constantly thinking I was going to die or get a disease. I became paranoid of the smallest things like a mosquito bite, which in my head could be a poisonous spider bite or an infection that would lead to death, and so on. This got me to a point where I was terrified to even leave home.

This followed me around for many years. I could have extreme panic attacks from thinking I had a disease, or I was going to die. This specific summer, I would just finish fifth grade. I was eleven years old. My hypochondriac moments were worse than ever.

This summer, my mom met the "man of her dreams." I thought so too.

My mom met Ben on a night out. Soon after, they moved in together. I really thought this was going to be everything I had ever wished for. I now had two stepsisters, and we became one big family. In the beginning, it was everything I had ever dreamed of. We had cozy dinners, went on vacations together and financially, it was better. My mom did not have to work double or triple shifts anymore to put food on the table. But as time went by, small things started to change. My home slowly became a war.

When I look back thinking about this period of my life, I can clearly see all the signs. I was only eleven years old. I did not think people would just be mean for no reason. I learned the hard way they could.

I never had a dad, so for me it was amazing to have a bigger family and a male role model in my life. I wanted my mom to work less and of course, to be happy.

They had dated for a short while before they decided to move in together. I would say it was about four months until we gave up our apartment and moved in. My big brother who is six years older than me, kept my mother's apartment, while we moved. Luckily for him, he never had to live in that house.

My heart was broken because I had to give away my guinea pigs, which were my best friends. I saw them as family members. I had them for over four years, but because he told my mom he was allergic to animals, they could not come with us. I was devastated, but I had to do as I was told, or we could not move.

It turned out to be a big lie. He just hated animals. He used to tell stories about how he tortured animals when he was younger as a fun joke. In fact, he used to joke about people's disabilities, like it was something to make fun of; showing videos of people with handicaps and laughing out loud. This was when we realized this man was not normal. He made us feel sick when he was telling his jokes. We had to tell him to stop, but he did not understand how we could not laugh with him. We were the crazy people, who were boring.

Things in our house started to escalate quickly after we moved in.

Ben was a tall, big man. He had served in the military. He was "always right" in every situation. He had strict rules, and everyone had to follow them, or there would be consequences. Control was one of his biggest issues. He liked manipulating you to believe anything he said. I remember feeling annoyed at first about his rules for everything in the house.

After a time, it became normal, like it had always been that way. In the beginning, I thought this was absolutely ridiculous, but as it became more and more of an everyday routine, I slowly accepted his rules and I (it)became normal.

Calling from the home phone was a problem I remember, and every day he went through the phone line to check on the numbers that had been called.

Our daily routines started to be controlled to a point where you did not know what was normal anymore. He had limited the time for taking a shower; ten minutes was the rule. Not because of the warm water, but due to the fact, mold could grow on the bathroom walls in the future. Even though it was a bathroom, which was built to handle water.

Every day, he was banging on the door and screaming. I was always in a rush and never knew what to expect at home. Getting out was the only option, or I would be grounded. A normal thing such as taking a shower became a big stressor you wanted to avoid at all costs. I used to skip taking showers sometimes, just to save myself from the anxiety that came from it.

He was a drinker, as well. In the beginning, it was only on the weekends, but then he started to hide drinks everywhere in the house and slowly, he was drinking almost every day. While he was drinking, he became more aggressive and acted out everything he was annoyed about. I felt extremely uncomfortable being alone with him in the house. I would always leave if it was just him and I, when my mom was at work.

Usually, he would take a nap in the middle of the day because he was too drunk to stay awake. My mom and I would be walking around on our toes trying not to make a sound, so we would not wake him up. This was the only time my mom and I were able to actually spend time together because we were not allowed to be alone together, at all. But we were terrified we might wake him up. If you woke him up, home would become a war.

At one time, I asked my mom, "Is this normal, do you think other people do this too, in their homes?" We both just looked at each other; that is when we knew how bad it really was.

When he was asleep, it was the only time my mom and I could speak to each other, because we were not allowed to speak in private. He used to say if we had anything to say, we could say it in front of him.

There was always screaming and fighting in our home. Still to this day, I do not understand how our neighbors never called the cops. It was seriously like a war. Every day it was something new, something I did that he needed to put my mom into her place for. My TV was too loud in my room, or I showered too long. One time, he was furious because one of the kitchen drawers was slightly open. He grounded me for that as well.

I forgot my plate from my breakfast one time in the living room. My mom begged me not to eat in there anymore. At the time, I was so mad at her for it. I felt like she took his part and stood behind whatever he said. But what I did not know, was he abused her with the same plate I had left by mistake in the living room. He beat her with the plate several times in her abdomen. He wanted to prove a point he said; to make her realize how useless I was. He threatened to kill her with the plate; he threatened, if I ever ate in there again, he would throw me out of the house. Of course, she was terrified. That was the reason she begged me not to eat in there again, to protect me.

You might think, what did my mom say or do against all of these crazy things he did? The truth is, she did step up in the beginning, but she was punished for it every time. After a while, it was normal for both of us, so we changed the way we lived, so he would not be upset or hurt us. I started to think about the smallest things, like not leaving the drawers out or placing the mayonnaise in the wrong holder in the refrigerator.

I used to sit in my room holding my pillow over my ears crying, while he and my mom were fighting. I was always scared of what I would see if I walked out of my room. Or if it became quiet, that was the worst. Then, I would run out just to see if my mom was hurt. My biggest fear was to find she had been injured.

I had many nightmares throughout this period, but one specific dream I had repeatedly was where I would find my mom dead. It was the exact same dream over and over. I would dream I woke up in the middle of the night to go into the kitchen looking for mom, but I could not find her. Then, I would go through the whole house searching for her, but she was nowhere to be found. Finally, when I opened the balcony door, there she was, laying in the snow with blood all over. I had these nightmares for several years, and even after we left, the same dream would happen again and again.

I told my mom about my nightmare. It freaked her out as well. She tried to cover everything up at this time, and was even lying to me. I saw bruises on her a lot. I always confronted her about them; she always blamed them on work. She worked as a casher in a supermarket. There is no way she got those bruises at work. I knew all along, but we both lived a lie for many years, covering it up.

No one around us could imagine how bad it was. From the outside, he was a super friendly man everyone liked. However, sometimes he would switch from being Mr. Nice Guy to Mr. Crazy Guy in just a millisecond. Even when his daughters came home, as soon as one of them opened the door, he switched his tone and became friendly. It was like living with two people and you never knew which one you were going to get.

It was embarrassing to bring friends home from school. I only did so a few times. Around the house, he had marked several walls with his fists when he was angry. Big holes which he tried to cover up. His reactions from when he was angry would go from hitting the walls to destroying things around the house or to hitting my mom. I remember how I never wanted to stay away from home in fear something would happen to her when I was gone.

It became a hard situation for me. I always felt like I was responsible for her. If I was there, he could never hurt her. Many times, my mom and I had to run away from home because it became unbearable. We had to pack everything we could in bags, then we ran away to hide at our friend's house. One time, we took shelter at my grandmother's house. We would stay there until he convinced my mom to come back.

When we ran away, we swore we were never going back again. However, my mom always went back in fear of what he would do if she did not listen to him. My closest friend Pillan was the only one who knew what was going on. She was there a few times to see his worst side.

One time, he threatened to throw her out of the house. We were late home that night. Pillan and I were around fourteen years old. We tried to convince my mom to let Pillan stay the night at my house. He came out to let us know it was not okay. He was screaming she had to leave. He gave her two minutes to get out of the house.

It was late at night and she lived far away. Her mother needed to come and pick her up, but we had no time to even call her. Pillan had to literally leave the house in two minutes. I decided to run out with her, so she did not have to stand alone outside in the dark, cold winter. He was punching the wall and screaming, "Get the fuck out of my house, you idiot." We had no choice, but to run away from him.

This was the first time I ran away from home. We stayed the night at a friend's house. The only thing I thought about that night was how badly my mom was punished because of me running away.

I cannot decide if being at home or being away from home was the worst—not knowing what was going on in the house while I was gone, and not being able to protect my mother, in case he went too far. It was a time of constant stress and anxiety.

My house was always a war. As I read my diary, I realized there were so many incidents written during this time. There was one where he took my food away in the kitchen. The dinner rule was also a huge thing. If you came home late, you would not get to eat food and you always needed to ask permission to eat. One time, he was having one of his naps, and I was super hungry because earlier I had been late for dinner, so I was not allowed to eat. I took this moment to act and made myself a sandwich and a glass of milk.

Suddenly, I heard his footsteps coming into the kitchen; I froze. I knew I was in big trouble. He was furious. He took the food, threw it in the trash, and screamed in my face.

He was so furious because I was eating. Just a normal thing such as having food in your own house was not allowed. As he started to completely lose his temper, he ran into the bathroom where my mom was taking the limited ten-minute shower, screaming her useless kid is eating, when she is not supposed to.

While he was in there, I grabbed a small kitchen knife and put it in my sweatpants pocket, just in case he would go over the line, which he often did. I was so scared. I did not know what to expect; all I knew was I needed to be ready, in case things escalated. As I walked out of the kitchen to go to my room, he came after me screaming "You little useless piece of shit," and as a reply, out comes the word "bastard," which made him run after me. I ran into my room, slammed the door and jumped onto my bed.

He opened the door, ran to my bed and jumped on top of me, grabbing my shirt and knocking me into the wall, over and over. I screamed at the top of my lungs, screaming for my mom. I grabbed the knife I had put in my sweatpants pocket earlier, trying to wave with it, so he would let me go. It made him go even crazier. He tried to take the knife from me as he was hitting my head into the wall.

My mom arrived in the room screaming. When she saw I had a knife, she tried to get me to throw it to her, while he was trying to grab the knife from me telling me to give it to him. Luckily, I managed to throw it to my mom. I do not know what would have happened if he was able to grab it.

The whole situation was out of hand. He finally let go of me, and I somehow managed to run out of the room and out of the house without any shoes. Barefoot in the snow, I ran to a friend who lived close by, where I could stay for a while until I had the courage to call my mom.

When I called my mom, she told me I needed to go straight home, and she would meet me halfway. As we walked home, she said I had to apologize to him. Today, I know she did not have a choice, but at that moment, I felt so alone. How could she be on his side, over and over again?

How can she stand by his side after everything he put us through?

She did not have a choice. I was so terrified to walk home that night. I did not know how to protect myself anymore. It was probably the worst night and week of my life. He told me this was the worst thing anyone had ever done to him. I was grounded for a month, and the atmosphere in the house was even worse than before.

I will never forget this moment; for me, it was the worst thing he did. I tried to protect myself with the worst possible item, but I was afraid for my life. Not only this time, but many times.

The terror was not only at daytime. Several times, I woke up in the middle of the night to find him beside my bed, staring at me. I developed a fear of sleeping at night, afraid of him getting into my room. Even today, I wake up from hearing the slightest sound. My mom could not sleep well at night either. She would wake up to find he was gone. When this happened, she immediately ran to find him in my room. She became very upset every time this happened. His answer was always," I am just looking."

"Looking for what?"

"Just looking…"

I never got an answer why he did this so often. It made me feel very uncomfortable. I started to be scared. Maybe he had done something while I was asleep, which was not possible, but maybe it was just a matter of time until he would. I will never know.

Many times, he even came into the bathroom when I was taking a bath, with the excuse of the "time-limit." It was very uncomfortable.

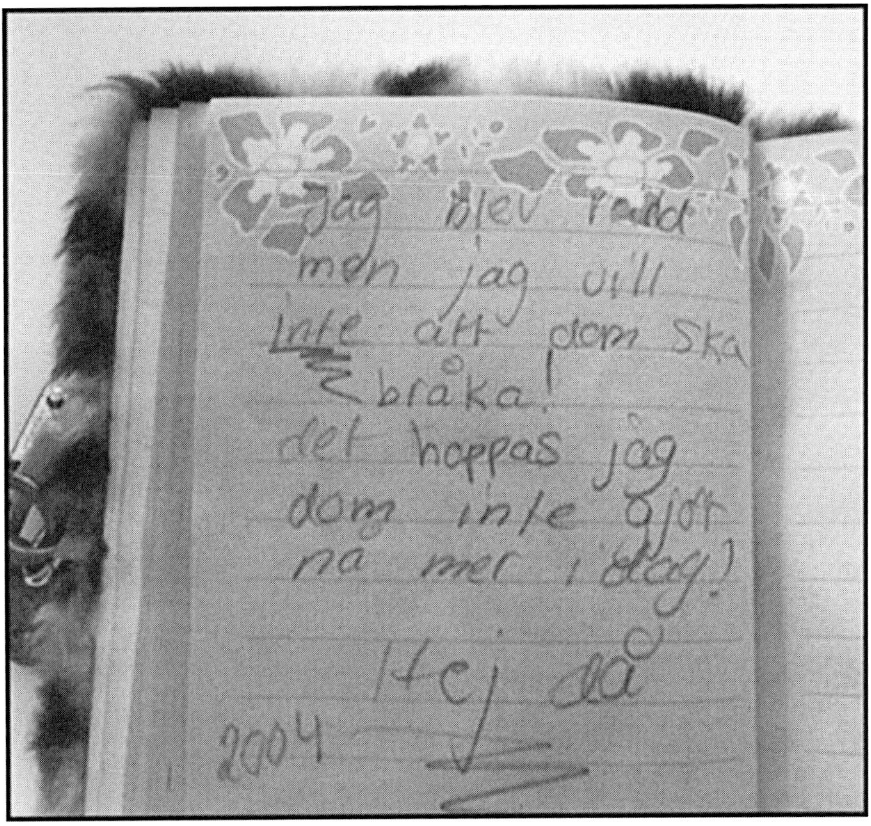
Jag blev rädd
men jag vill
inte att dom ska
bråka!
det hoppas jag
dom inte gjör
na mer i dag!
Hej då
2004

så stort

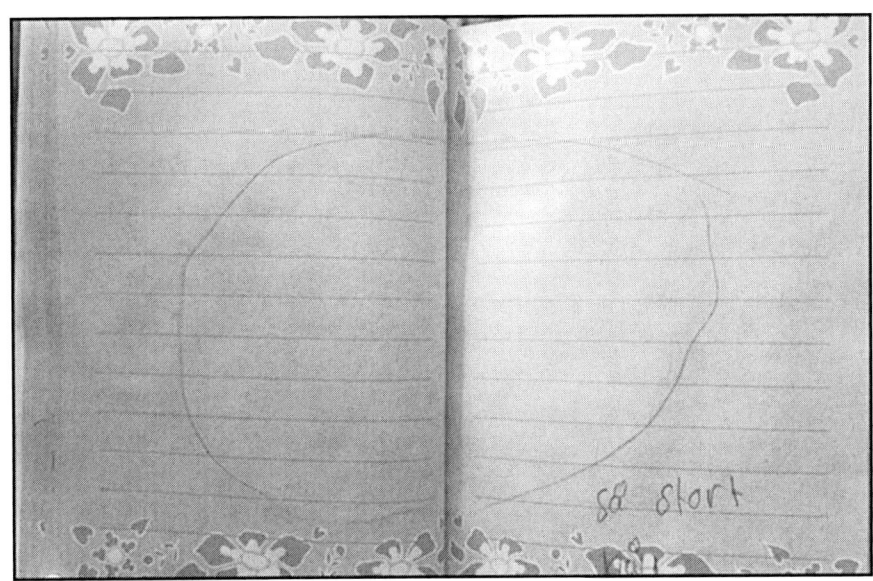

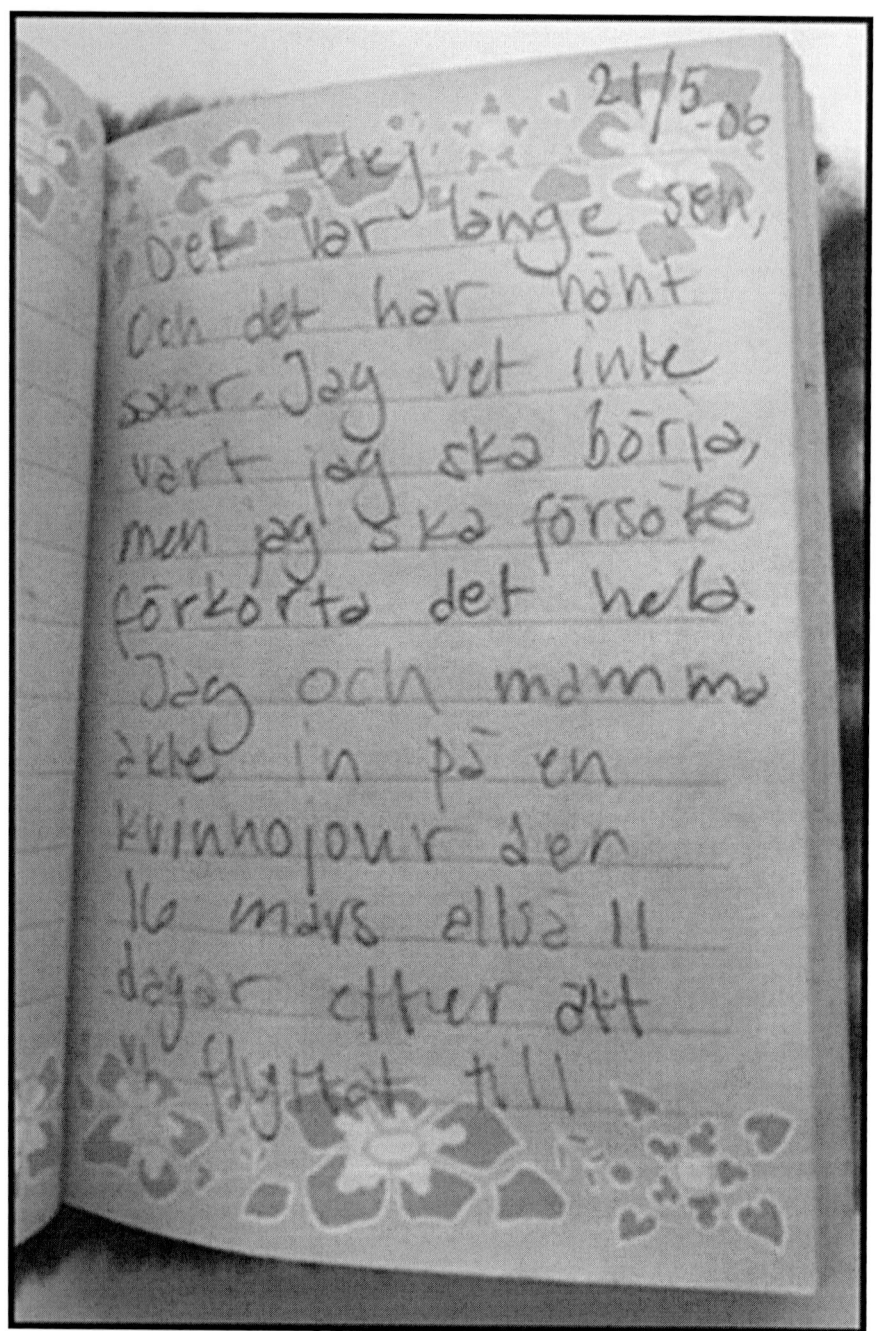

21/5 -06

Hej
Det har länge sen,
och det har hänt
saker. Jag vet inte
vart jag ska börja,
men jag ska försöke
förkorta det hela.
Jag och mamma
äkte in på en
kvinnojour den
16 mars elba 11
dagar etter att
vi flyttat till

CHAPTER III:

The Start of a Never-Ending Fight

Finally, it came to a point where I told my mom we needed to get out of the house. We had talked about it many times, but nothing really happened. It was not until I told her a lie, a lie that would save our lives. –The social service will take me away from you if we do not move.

I told my mom I had spoken with a teacher at school about how things actually were in our home. I said I told the teacher I did not feel safe, and I had a stomach ache every time I went home. It was not a total lie. I mentioned it, but only very briefly with a school counselor. She did not discuss the social service at all. I just knew if I talked about the "social service" that my mom would become scared and might have the courage to take some action.

I am glad I did, as it was the turning point for her. She did everything in her power to get an apartment. So, there we were, my mom and I, having this big secret behind his back, trying to find a new place to live.

Every Tuesday and Thursday, I had to have a note for school saying I had to leave earlier from school. This was so I could get the mail before he came home. It was 2005, and to get the answer from the apartment company, you had to wait for a letter to come in the mail, to see if you got the apartment or not.

Back in 2005, we had to apply for an apartment online and get the answers by mail. I had to run home after school to see if we had any news. After months of waiting and applying for apartments, we finally received the letter we had been waiting for; we had an apartment.

When the day came for my mom to tell him we were moving, he lost his mind. He chased her and pulled a knife to her throat, telling her she could never get away from him, so it was no point for her to try. He was not going to let her go that easy. He made it very clear.

He forced my mom to tell him exactly where the apartment was, so he would know where we would be moving. He forced her into the car to make her point out the exact house we were going to move into. Somehow, he was able to trade the apartment we lived in for another apartment, just a house away from where we were going to move. This is the craziest part of the story. He did everything he could, to destroy our lives, but also to keep controlling us.

We all moved on the same day, March 4th, 2006, to different apartments, but on the same street. It is ironic how this man accomplished all this and how he refused to let us move on with our lives. We lived in our new apartment for sixteen days until it became unbearable. In those sixteen days, he slowly moved back in. He put an extra bed in our apartment, along with his clothes. He was in our apartment all day and was giving orders just like he had done before.

He left four bagels in the kitchen one morning. I ate two of them. I thought it was mom who had bought them, but they were actually his "bagels." When he found out, he raised his voice and threw the remaining bagels at me, screaming I was a piece of shit for eating his bagels. My only reply was, "This is our home, and if you leave things here, I take it as if they belong to me as well." He became so mad; he dragged my mom into his apartment. Forcing her to stay. This went on and on, and slowly my mom lived in his apartment. At the very end, he locked her in his apartment for two whole days. After those two long days, we fled for our lives to a woman's shelter to get help.

This was our turning point, but it was also the start of a whole other chapter of fighting for our rights and to get the help we needed. He was out there walking around as a free man and we needed to hide for months. It was like we were prisoners. We could barely go out to buy groceries. I remember feeling so little. There was nothing I could do.

My mom was terrified and refused to leave the women's shelter at any time. We needed to get help with everything from shopping to cooking. She was scared every time she saw a white car, because he had a white car. Even when she heard a man's voice, she would freeze and become anxious. She started to be so paranoid. The smallest little thing would send her into a panic attack. I was in the middle trying to be a grown-up. As a fourteen-year old, that was a lot of responsibility on my shoulders.

Leaving Ben, to start a new life and fighting for our rights to get the help to move forward was everything, but easy. It was like the start of a never ending-fight.

There we were, inside a women's shelter we now called our "new home", not knowing for how long we needed to stay or what we were going to do after. We had nothing, but the clothes we had on and the few things we took with us the day we left. I did not go to school for three months. I felt like a prisoner. I could not tell anyone where I was or why I was away. I missed my school, my friends, and especially, my freedom. A whole other chapter now began, of fighting for our rights within the system and trying to start a new life.

Time went by and the trial came up. Going through all the changes was a struggle by itself. But having to see him after all this time and after everything he put us through, was a rollercoaster of feelings. I felt scared and of course, I was angry. I was angry for all the things he'd put me through, but also for all those horrible things he put my mother through, which was clear to me now.

When we finally got away from him, mom and I could now openly talk to each other, which gave her time to tell me all the stories she had kept from me throughout those years. I knew all along he was a horrible person, but the things she had been through, were just over the top. I understood then why my mother had been "on his side" and told me so many times to apologize even if I did not do anything wrong. It was to protect me; not her. He could do whatever he wanted to her, but when he started threatening to do things to me, she did whatever she needed to do to keep me safe.

At the trial, we had no evidence. It was our word against his word, that is why in cases like domestic violence it is super hard to prosecute the abuser. Where is the evidence? We had no pictures of the bruises or the walls, neither did we have anything on film. Only our stories. But we got through it. He received probation and a restraining order. We felt relieved after the trial knowing he had a restraining order, but we could still meet him at any time. We did not feel safe or protected. We still lived in the same city, just a few miles away from him.

We were alive. But Mom and I needed to start a whole new life. My mom was not able to take care of me or herself at this time. I was around fifteen years old and needed to grow up fast. My relationship with her was unstable. She was a wreck and she was not able to leave the house by herself for a long time, for fear of meeting him. She was fragile and was mostly sleeping all day long. She was completely broken down, and trying to be the parent was not something she could do at this time.

We tried our best, living under the same roof. However, our relationship became worse after our trauma together with Ben. I found my cure with alcohol and my first "real boyfriend."

I got into deep water with this guy. He was a typical "bad boy." He was the popular guy everyone wanted to be with, but he was also jealous, controlling and dangerous. He was my first relationship. I had nothing else to compare this to. He came to use me in so many ways. I was fifteen and he was eighteen. I was so in love. I thought he could make this period of my life so much better, but in fact, he made it so much worse. We were dating for three months when I first moved in with him to a small apartment. At the age of fifteen, this was an incredibly bad decision.

He always knew how to get his way by comparing me to his ex-girlfriend. Everything I said "NO" to or did not want to do, he used her to convince me. "Emelie would have done it, or Emelie always did that" he used to say. I was already a broken teenager with low self-esteem, and this did not help at all. Using this "Emelie would do it" got me to do many things I was really uncomfortable with and did not want to do at all, some of them, sexual.

Today, I know Emelie would never have done those things he convinced me to do. It was his way of controlling me. I wanted to make him happy, so he would keep loving me or at the very least, love me as much as Emelie. His personality, wishes and desires were so above mine that it got to a point where I no longer existed. I lost myself completely.

Thinking to myself: "Am I really the one that is wrong all the time? Was this fighting really because of me?". My head burned out. It was always my fault in every situation. We used to have big fights, and we broke up many times, only to get back together; it was a toxic relationship. The psychological abuse and taking sexual advantage of me became worse. At one time, he raped me.

I remember at Halloween; he almost broke my nose with his forehead. We were at a Halloween party, and we had all been drinking. I think he had taken cocaine that night. We got into an argument. I was sitting down on the stairs inside the house where the party was being held. He wanted me to look him in the eye and when I did, he leaned forward and knocked me with his forehead on my nose.

My nose started to bleed. I could not believe what had just happened. Everyone around me was in shock, including me. People at the party tried to get him away from me, as he was trying to punch a hole in the door beside me. I was crying and terrified. My friend was trying to get me out of the house, and we hid in the neighbor's garage.

People around him feared and respected him because he was dangerous, and that is how he wanted it.

Finally, after almost two years of this toxic relationship, I made up my mind. I needed to get away from this guy. I did not want to follow in my mother's footsteps. When my mom and I moved to a new town, I had the chance to break up with him and get away, but he did not think it was a good idea. Instead, he started to hunt me with threatening text messages. One specific text he wrote was, "You should watch your back, when you walk around." "You should watch out for acid."

That text freaked me out so much I had problems leaving the house in fear he would send someone to do such a thing to me. He also told me "I will send a group of people to come and get you; I will lock you in the basement and you will be a sex slave." Insane threats which luckily never happened, but I was terrified and it led me to become paranoid.

I did not want to leave the house, and every time I did, I was always looking many times over my shoulder. In a selfish way, I hoped he found another girlfriend, so he would stop harassing me. He finally did, and I moved on to a better, much healthier relationship.

CHAPTER IV:

Before It Became Better
It Got Worse

I would say living in a "war behind closed doors" is mentally and physically draining, but the life afterwards was even worse. For a long time afterwards, my mom was psychologically degraded and scared of everything. Our relationship was destroyed, after so many years without really talking or having a relationship. There was tension between us. We had huge fights, where I usually left home. I was an angry, scared and confused teenager. I did not know how to handle all of these emotions which came up after the traumas. At fifteen, I was a rebel trying to fight my own demons with alcohol and drugs.

I ran away from home when all I really did was try to run away from myself and my feelings, which I never really took responsibility for. It should be no surprise that I met my boyfriend who I had a super toxic relationship with. My mom could see from miles away it was a bad relationship. She forbade me to see this guy. For a long time, I met him behind her back.

The fact I barely could make my way through eighth grade because I could not go to school while being in the woman's shelter, made me think of quitting everything, but I managed to stay all the way through. I studied extra after school. I did summer school between the eighth and ninth grade, so I would get the grades I needed to apply for a theater and TV high school I really wanted to go to.

After I had completed a tryout and went on an audition, I was accepted to that high school. It was the start of something new and positive for me. I was able to put my energy into something I really loved, theater. I met new friends. Since this was in a new city, I got away from the old city. For me, it was a new start. Even though high school was super hard for me, I was usually feeling tired, but I did my best. Once a week, my mom and I went to family therapy with the hope of restoring our relationship.

In my second year of high school, I experienced a long period of depression, feeling down and unmotivated to really do anything. I remember sitting on the bus one day after school. It was winter; dark days and very cold. I was thinking there must be something more than this to life. I had one of those down periods, where life was absolutely meaningless.

Having fear for the future, should I stay here forever, is this really how I want my life? I just wanted whatever was out there in this big world, except being stuck in the same city with the same people. I was looking for a change. As a confused seventeen-year old, I was thinking I needed to do something with my life. I looked up at the bus-window, and I saw this sign, a commercial sign. It said, "Go study abroad with STS exchange student program."

It was a clear sign for me; it was destiny. There I was thinking about how can I make my life more meaningful? And then I see this commercial, I just needed to look it up. I did, as soon as I arrived home. This is when I decided I was going to be an exchange student. However, my grades were not good enough to even make it into the program, so I had to work really hard on getting them back up.

Months later after going through interviews, tests and working on my grades, I received an email. I had finally been chosen by a family, who lived in Houston, Texas.

This was one of my escapes, which was super healthy for me to move on and get away from all the reality back in Sweden. Plus, it gave mom and I a break from each other. She really thought it was a great idea when I told her about my plan of being an exchange student. Starting to work hard for my goals created more positive feelings. Life was actually good, much better than in a long time.

That year in Texas, taught me so many things. One bonus was I got a new family for life. I grew so much with the family I stayed with because they really showed me how good life could be. They showed me how a functional family worked. I felt like a family member while living there. I experienced the best days of my life. Life there was like in the movies.

I was so sure I was going to end up there, get married and just start a life over there; that was my goal for a long time. I did not want to go back to Sweden at all. I knew I needed to go back to finish school, and of course, I missed my brother, my mom, and my friends.

When I came back to Sweden, I came back as a better me. I had grown a lot as a person and I think my family really saw that and appreciated it. I was eighteen when I came back to finish my last year of high school. My mom could easily tell I had become more mature. But coming back to "reality" with all the old people and memories, made me go back into a bad spiral again. Slowly, I was starting to feel depressed again, and new plans of running away came to my mind.

While being in Sweden, the beginning of the documentary "Say Something" started to take place. Mom and I decided to tell our story through a documentary. The company was called, *Film and Tell*. They had a mission of showing the real life of a family who had been broken from abuse and their life afterwards. They followed our lives for five years, but they only recorded once in a while. It was not like they lived in our house recording every step we took. It was more like a short-term filming to catch the life between my mom and me.

We volunteered because we wanted to help others by telling our story and the goal was to change how the system in Sweden was built for cases like ours. We struggled so much getting help from the social services. Everything was a fight because we were told we cost society too much and we needed to figure out things on our own.

But how? My mother was a wreck; destroyed, scared and paranoid. I was a child who did not know what to do or how to deal with my own emotions. Just simple things as, how do you get from a women's shelter to a new home? How do you start all over and how can you get help to do so? Who is going to pay when the mother cannot go to work due to the security of her life? How can the children still be educated when they cannot go to school? The questions were many and we had to figure things out. We found so many holes in the system.

The documentary "Say Something" was born and so was my self-destructive behavior. I was drinking every chance I could, taking drugs and feeling depressed. My anxiety was completely destroying me. I did everything, to not feel anything. I knew I had to deal with some things I had never really dealt with before. I just went on with life as if the things I had been through never happened. It was easier that way.

Yes, sometimes I talked about it, but I always wanted to be strong and replied with something like, "it was in the past, and it is over, why do we need to talk about it?" But inside of me, it kept going on and on. Emotionally, I was drained, and what I really needed, was to get help. Dealing with my emotions and going through the anger I was feeling. Not denying or pushing everything forward, because sooner or later it would catch up with me. All I wanted was for it to be over and even if it was, it still haunted me inside.

I went back to Texas after my last year of high school. I wanted to go back with the hope of starting my own life there. I was going to be there for three months. Instead of creating a decent living so I could stay, I partied and lived life on the edge. I spent time being around friends who took a drug called "White Horse", which was a stimulant drug like cocaine. At this time, it was legal in Texas, and you could buy it at the tobacco store. "White Horse" was the drug known as "bath salts."

I was curious and when using it made me lose weight, I was hooked. I could not stop, and I was terrified to gain the weight back. I was never big, but I always wanted to lose an extra seven kilos. I just never had the determination to do so; this was my quick fix. This drug took me to places emotionally I had never been before.

It was not in a good way; it was quite the opposite. I started to hallucinate, which created an anxiety which had me thinking about killing myself to escape the horrible feelings. I could not go to sleep. I was up for days. At one time, I had been up for four days straight. I lost my mind. I saw things that were not there. I started to laugh uncontrollably, and my body started to move involuntarily. It was scary.

Trying to sleep while being high was like trying to force yourself to die. I had so many nervous feelings. To be able to sleep, I usually had to take something to bring me down, like a painkiller or a sleeping pill. Sometimes I could stay awake, staring into absolutely nothing the whole night long, which slowly drove me insane. At one point, I did not know what was real and what was not.

Did the people around me really notice I was different and high, thinking I was a weirdo? It felt like it. I started to have visions about people not liking me and that they were out to get me. I was so paranoid. I thought people were stalking me or even following me around. I was terrified people around me could see I was high. Or they had thoughts of me being weird. I know today, I had gotten a psychosis.

I had no clue then; I thought it was reality. I remember having panic attacks, and because of the anxiety I could not eat. It was like I was about to puke every time I put something in my mouth, while I was high. At one time, I fainted and fell right down on the floor. I should have seen it as a sign to stop, but I kept going. Starving myself and trying to take "White Horse" as often as I could, so I would not binge eat. I was so malnourished when I stopped taking the drug; I stuffed my face with food. I had no control over my binge eating.

I remember thinking, would I ever feel "normal" again? Will the anxiety ever go away? I started to count how long I stared people in the eyes, so I would not stare at them for too long. At this point, I was so paranoid that anyone around me could probably see it. I made the decision to take White Horse, as an escape, but all it did was make me worse than ever. Family around me tried to help and make me stop, but it was too late. I needed to fly back to Sweden.

Being back in Sweden after this was complete chaos. This is where my worst time began. To be able to deal with both my paranoid thoughts and emotions, I needed alcohol to feel calm and sleeping pills to go to sleep. I was admitted to the hospital in the psychiatric care section a couple of times. Mostly when I was extremely drunk and aggressive, wanting to kill myself.

My friends back home noticed before I even noticed that I needed help, or I might lose my life. I made bad decisions and those choices led me to be in situations that could have been very dangerous for me. This went on for about a year after I had come home from the United States. I went on an escape trip to Thailand, all by myself. Traveling and being alone were things that helped me feel better, but only for the moment.

Even if too much alone time almost broke me into pieces, I needed it in small portions, to recharge my battery. However, I was drunk and partied way too much while I was there. I woke up one morning turning onto my side. I saw I had plastic around my arm. I then discovered; I had gotten a tattoo the night before.

I had no memories at all about this, and on my arm, it said: "I fucked up again." For 2 weeks, I thought it was a henna tattoo, but I came to realize, it was not. In my drunken stupor, I had gotten a drunken tattoo. It should have been a sign to stop, but instead, I just made fun of it, and kept drinking.

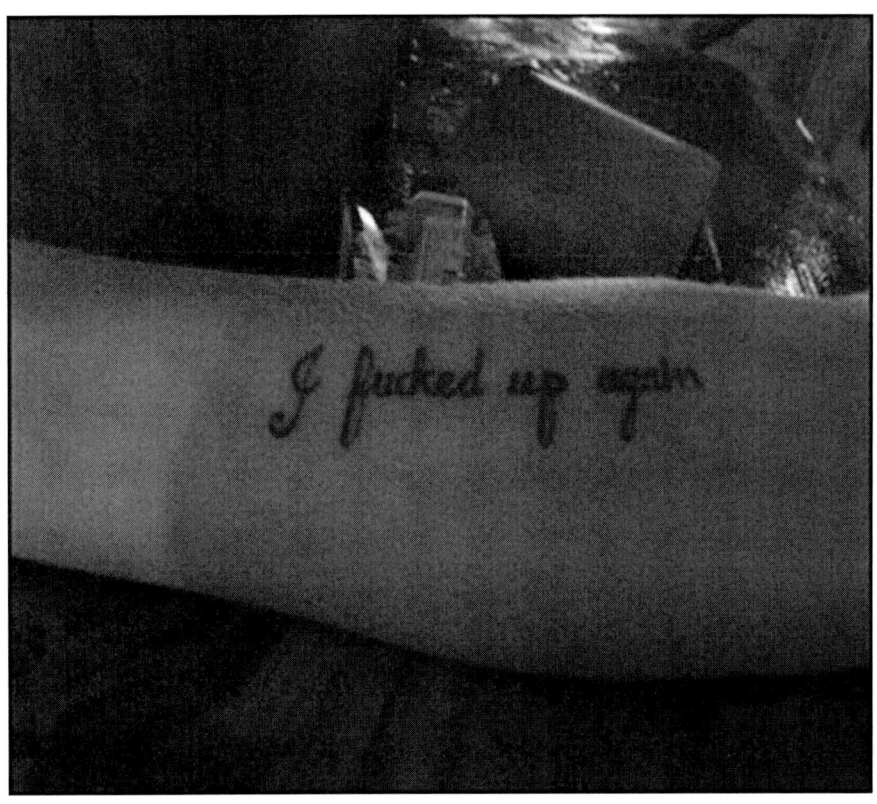

At this point in my life, anything that could make my anxious feelings go away was a perfect escape. It felt like I was a prisoner in my own body trying to constantly run from myself.

One time, I was drinking during the day and when night came, I was so drunk and depressed. I had problems with anxiety for a long while. Drinking made those feelings even stronger. I was basically in one of my bad states, where everything was bad, dark and nothing really mattered anymore. I wanted to end my life, to stop the pain. I wanted to release myself from all of the misery.

One of my close friends and I were at a get together party. I was ready to leave, I felt anxious and needed to get out of there before anyone could tell. As my friend and I were outside to cross the road to take the bus home, I stopped and tried to get hit by a car. I was saved that night by both the driver and my friend. The ambulance came, and they took me into psychiatric care.

CHAPTER V:
Silver Lining

I think it was the fifth time in a very short period that I landed back in the psychiatric hospital. I had two choices; get help or destroy myself. I met a great psychologist. She had me sitting in a chair talking about everything which had happened over the last year, about the drugs I used, the paranoid thoughts and my drinking habits. Sitting there made me understand it was not the last year that had made me this bad. It was the drugs which brought out the worst in me. All the things I was trying to forget for so many years had caught up with me. I had a psychosis as a result of not facing my feelings or my past.

We needed to find a way to get me back up on my feet. I knew I could not live like this anymore; I wanted to change, but I did not know how. I knew it was going to be hard, but I also knew I needed to go through the emotions I had been pushing away for years. I had been running from them for such a long time. I was nineteen, about to turn twenty, and when I pictured my future, it was not like this. I pictured myself in the future being successful, balanced and not in pain; completely the opposite from the way I felt at that precise moment. The psychologist asked me if I needed help to stop drinking alcohol.

I did.

Just the thought of not being able to drink, to take my anxiety away when I wanted to, scared me so much. But I had no other choice. She told me about a "medication" called "Antabus" which could help me, but it was more like a substitute. I was supposed to take it for a while to help me to stay away from alcohol.

Antabus is a drug used to support the treatment of chronic alcoholism by producing an acute sensitivity to ethanol (drinking alcohol). Antabus does not reduce alcohol cravings, but it helps because if you drink while on the medication, you get incredibly sick. I knew I would not take the chance of getting sick, so I would not drink alcohol at all if I took this medication. I knew this was the only choice, so I started to take Antabus.

They also put me on a medication called "Seroquel Depot" for my psychosis and bipolar disorder. The doctor and the psychologists suspected I was bipolar and made me go through a psychological investigation where I had to do tests, answer questions and go to regular meetups. They came to the conclusion I was Bipolar type II. For years, I believed it too. I kept taking the medication for my bipolar disorder for years, without even knowing what the medication was doing to my body or my mind. I just trusted the doctors.

When I was released from the hospital, after the car incident, I was ready to keep fighting my inner demons on my own, out in the real world. Quitting the alcohol made me see things clearer, I finally wanted to do something more with my time and my life. Even if it was hard facing my emotions and talking about the past, I was determined to get through this. It got me much further in life than I ever was before; I felt free. As time went by, I started to feel restless. Wanting to do something more productive with my time, I started going to the gym. It helped me to clear my mind, to get more energy and of course, to see results with my body.

Back when I was in Texas, doing drugs, I lost a lot of weight. This was the beginning of me having a very bad relationship with food, which made me be very careful with what I ate. When I had too much to eat, I forced myself to puke. It was a constant battle inside of me. I started developing bulimia.

I realized at this moment; how easy it was to switch one addiction to another. When I finally started to get rid of my biggest problem, alcohol, I started controlling my eating habits more and more. It started with me going every day to the gym, just to get a routine. Instead of eating well, I started to cut down on everything I ate, becoming obsessed with what and how much I ate. I started to lose weight very fast. Now my alcohol abuse had turned into a training obsession; I had replaced one addiction with another. I went from sixty-four kilos to forty-three kilos in six months. I had no idea at the time I had developed an eating disorder called anorexia. At my worst, I would have so much anxiety, just because I chewed too much gum in a day. I punished myself for hours in the gym or by walking.

I was walking hours and hours every day. Everything had to be organized around my training schedule. I could not do anything with friends or family until my training was done. My mom was terrified. I remember her saying, "Please it all needs to stop now. I do not want to lose you."

I had no idea how bad it was. I only saw a fat pig in the mirror. My scale needed to show me less and less to keep my demons satisfied. My diary from this period is where some of the worst self-hate is printed on those pages. I wrote things such as: I need to lose weight now, fast, no more food today. Out and run, you ugly shit. You will die from obesity. You could not say no to the last bite of food huh? You are disgusting. Maybe you should die, then at least no one need to see your ugly thighs anymore.

It brings me to tears to read this today. How can you do this to yourself? It is absolutely frightening that you would ever say something like that or think like that about yourself. My inner thoughts were these cruel and very big lies. I wish I had known back then what I know today.

Idag vinter jagpa mannmens. Den har inte kommit.
Jag tro den kommer för det känns. Så länge jag
har mens är det inge fel på kroppen. Så har
jag ätter. Skönt. Folk lägger sig i mer å mer
hur jag ser ut å väger. Johan säger inget om
min vikt å så länge han inte klagar så
är jag inte för smal. Jag känner mig jätte
svullen, går på Nutrilett å har gjort det
sen igår. Imorrn blir det wasa + kalke, Subway +
äpple. + Massa vatten. Jag hinner inte fråm
idag ÅNGEST! Men imorrn blir det hårdträning
ledig ons+Tors. Ska träna jätte mycket
hur jag ska slippa återsången på för eller
föresten, Skippar nästa istället. Måste gå
ner nu. Fan det går för långsamt. Måste

skit samma, Idag ä en bra dag
& jag försöker tänka positivt.
Inge mat tankar, inge ångest
& ska träna efter jobbet,
längtar även fast jag känner
mig som den fetaste ugglan
i hela mossen idag får
det inte förstöra den positiva
energin jag har idag.
Tror jag har bestämt mig för
att åka till Turkiet m johan
men jag blir så osäker, fan
tänk om jag får ångest, han
kommer försöka proppa
i mig mat & jag måste
ha på mig bikini ÅNGEST!
vill inte visa mig på nån
strand, kommer se ut som
en strandad val likblek
& fet.

Dom frågar hur man kan må dåligt
när man är så vacker.
Utifrån, har man allt. Ett leende som
lurar den bästa pokerproffset.
Insidan skriker og paranoian är på topp.
Ångesten är bara en av sidorna som är
jag. Ensamheten og tystnaden är så jävla
närvarande. Människors dömande ögon
är så vidriga. Hur kan ett utseende ge en
allt? Var är lyckan, skrattet og må bra
känslorna när jag behöver dem!
Ingen får se eller veta vad som
försiggår på insidan.
Allt jag vill är att få vara lycklig
iallafall minst må bra.
Ibland vet jag inte vad jag ska göra.

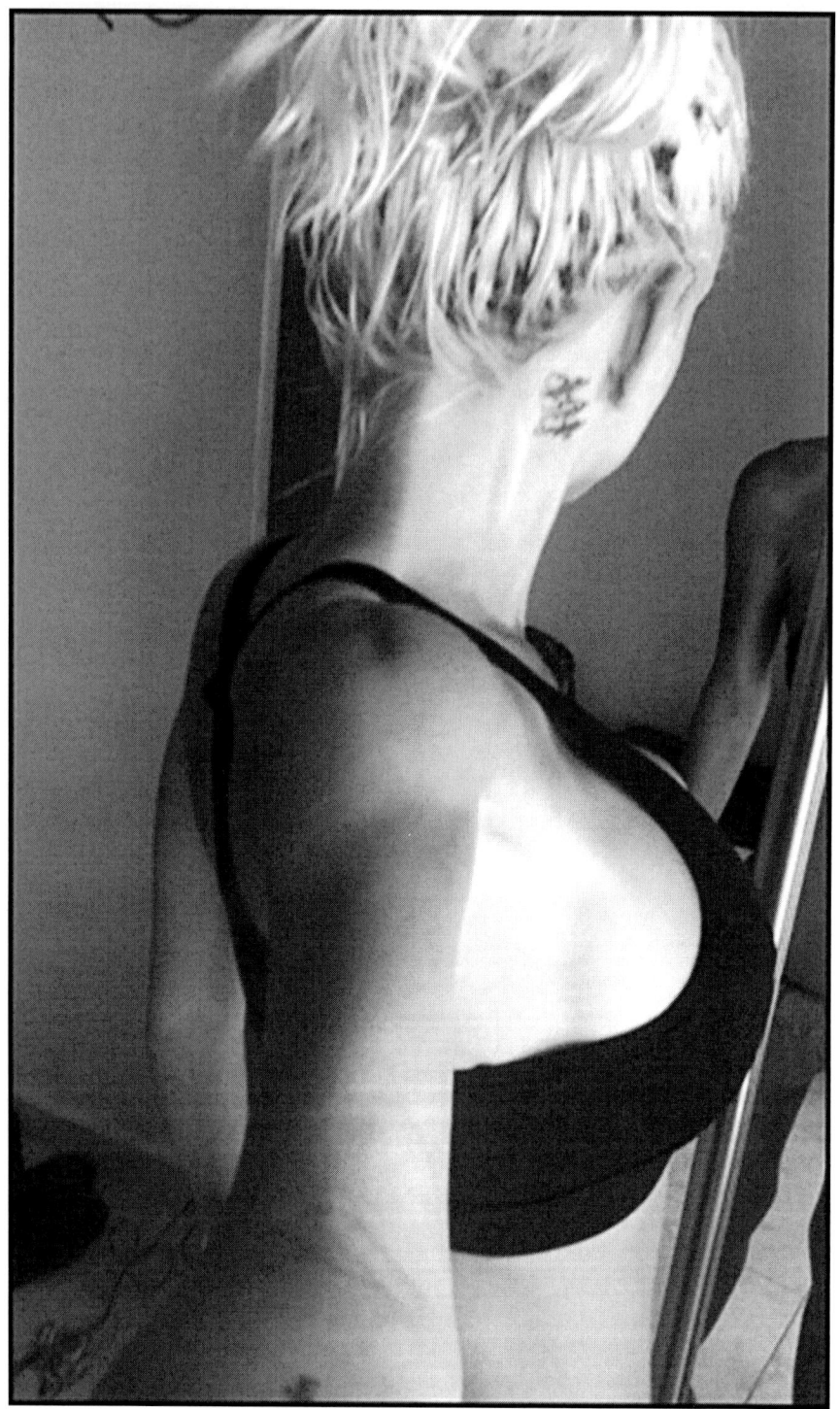

I remember having nightmares about eating, say a hamburger for example, could make me wake up in tears. Waking up all sweaty and going directly to weigh myself. I was feeling so insecure. I hated looking at myself in the mirror. It felt like I had two of "me" inside myself. One who knew I was sick and needed help and the other one who was never happy with the results. Sometimes, I knew I needed help. I even called a clinic one time. They wanted me to get there right away.

Then, I went back to feeling nothing, but disgusting, fat and hopeless. So, I went out for a long walk instead. At the same time, as I wanted to die, I did not want to die at all. I was terrified my heart would stop while being asleep.

Even if I was breaking myself down, I knew somehow, I was on the right track. One step at a time, the pieces fell into place. I knew, this is not how it is going to be forever. I was on a journey, and it would take time.

I later decided to move to Norway in a city called Stavanger. It all started because of the work I had at this time as a gold buyer and the company needed to expand and become bigger in Norway. I did a really good job in Sweden, so they recommended me to the manager in Stavanger (Norway). I got the opportunity to move in just a week. Starting a new adventure, I had said yes to, I packed my life into four big suitcases and bought my train ticket. Later, I moved in with the girl I had met on the train on my way to the new country. We became not only housemates but very close friends.

My eating disorder was taking the best of me; I was sick. At this point, I weighed forty-three kilos. Breaking apart inside, I knew something needed to change, so I moved. Stavanger was the new beginning for me. I met new people. I could be myself and not what I had been for many years. It was a new fresh start.

I started to lose my control while being there. Control over the gym hours and what I put into my mouth, so I started to gain weight very fast. I did not know how to stop it or keep it on a healthy level. I was freaking out, so instead of doing it the right way, I binged and purged almost every day. I had lost my routines, which scared me more than ever.

I could not stop eating, or that is what I felt like. I was hiding food everywhere, then I would eat it in secret and binge in the toilet. I was constantly talking about losing weight and in my head, it was the only thing I was thinking about. It was the opposite now; instead of starving, I could not stop eating. I tried to keep going to the gym, but every time I ate, I felt too bad to even go. I do not know if this period was even worse than the anorexia period. Now, I had developed bulimia.

In the middle of all this, I fell in love with my manager. We had a secret relationship for a short time. I was head over heels for this man. We used to talk for hours. I think I found him as a comfort, but I started to need him to a point that it became unbearable because of my eating disorder. He started to realize this, and I could tell he was trying to end the relationship. And in desperation, I was doing everything to keep him in my life. It became a cat and mouse "game." Where I lost big time. I was getting sicker and more self-destructive than ever. I slowly pushed him away. It ended without a real "ending" of the relationship which broke me into pieces. Instead of telling me he could not take it any longer, he stopped replying to my calls and my texts.

I did not know then, I had to take responsibility for my destructive behaviors. I needed to heal myself, instead of waiting for someone like him to come and save me. I was not his responsibility, neither was he to be blamed. At the time, I was already too deep in my own sadness and pity for myself, so, I did what I always did. I ran away.

One night, I was drunk and took a whole package of sleeping pills. My roommate found me while I was talking loudly to myself. The ambulance came and they had to flush my stomach, and I survived once again. The doctor told me I should have died that night and this time I was extremely lucky. Maybe it was time to change again?

A week after, I ended whatever was left of the relationship and moved back to Sweden. The only right thing for me to do was to go home, get more help and of course, be with my family who was worried about my condition.

I had not visited Sweden since I moved, which was for 11 months. My mom was happy when she realized I had gained weight, but nobody really knew how bad it actually was and how much I tried to lose it. I hid my disease as much as I could. For all I knew, it was normal to always want to lose weight. It was a part of my life, and that is how it had been for a long time. In fact, as long as I can remember, I have always tried to lose weight. Always watching what I ate, how I trained, what I wore, to look skinnier. Nothing was ever enough for my demons. It did not matter if I weighed forty-three kilos or seventy-five kilos, it was never enough.

In the middle of everything, I started to doubt myself. Can I really "fix" myself? Can I get out of this shit? I was heartbroken, lost, insecure, depressed and with an anxiety from hell. Why could not I just be happy, or at least normal or okay? What was wrong with me? Why was I so broken? It took me years to figure out I had all the possibilities to be okay, more than okay actually. I found happiness, satisfaction and balance.

Balance was the main key for me to find.

Later on, I had a vision; I wanted to travel the world. That became my next mission and my goal.

Get out there in the world, feeling free and find something else I could not find where I was in Sweden, in my little hometown Tyresö.

CHAPTER VI:

How Traveling
Changed My Life

To reach my goal of travelling the world, I needed money, a lot of it. So, there I was packing my bags again. This time I moved to Oslo, another city in Norway. I knew working in Norway would get me the money I needed. I worked at the airport for fourteen months in total. I had, at the most, four different jobs. A few times, I slept down in the arrivals, in one of my offices to get the time for sleep between shifts.

I was stubborn and I was driven. Even though I had my depression, I still wanted more out of life, always. If I wanted something, I would go after it, no matter how hard or far away it was. But sometimes, my emotions came in between and I fell down. I was used to it by now.

Working four jobs was a little overwhelming. I became sick and depressed. I kept pushing through the last three months. I hated every second of this time during my life. I am not going to lie; it was super hard. I worked almost seven days a week all these months and saved every penny I made. I knew what I wanted. It was going to be worth it.

On my birthday, November 30, 2014, my flight to Nairobi, Kenya, took off. My mom had begged me not to go because of the Ebola epidemic that was going around in certain parts of Africa. I was not planning on getting sick, so I told her, "You have to put your anxiety aside because I need to follow my dream no matter how bad it feels right now for you." That sentence is something she always brings up even today.

My mom said, "You really had me thinking when you said that. Thank you for telling me. I needed to hear it."

I went all by myself and even if it was scary, I knew doing this on my own would make me grow. I would be gaining so much from it. When I touched down in Nairobi, my anxiety became so strong I felt like dying. Maybe I needed to turn around and go back home. Would I really be able to do all this by myself? I went back and forth in my head. Everyone around me had told me I was crazy doing this on my own.

I felt like I was fooled by myself. What if I get kidnaped or I get a disease? No matter what I felt I had to keep moving forward. I was on a mission. I needed this for my growth, to move forward and be happy, right?

I was gone for eight months. I visited twenty-two countries and three continents. Here is a list of the places I went to:

Kenya	Botswana	Indonesia	Thailand
Tanzania	South Africa	Chile	Cambodia
Zambia	Brazil	Bolivia	Singapore
Malawi	Uruguay	Peru	Philippines
Namibia	Argentina	Vietnam	
Zimbabwe	Malaysia	Laos	

Throughout my travels, I kept a diary. I was writing to remember everything I tried, saw and experienced. I am so happy today, I kept writing in it because you forget faster than you think.

I spent around forty-five days in Africa, visiting eight countries. There was one specific incident I remember all too well because it changed my life forever. Just a couple of days before Christmas, I went to a city named Livingstone in Zambia.

A beautiful city with many adventures to try, like zip-line or bungy-jumping. I decided I was going to visit the Devil's pool which is a part over the amazing Victoria Falls. I also signed up to bungy-jump, basically jump off a bridge, a small platform on the Victoria Falls railway bridge, between the borders of Zambia and Zimbabwe.

That is where I decided to just jump off with all my fears, feelings and the baggage from my past I had carried for so long. Just to prove to myself, I could, even if it scared me to death. It took me two times of almost jumping, even if I backed off and they had to take off the cord off my legs two times. Because on the third time, I did it. I jumped off screaming like a baby, but I did it.

The people around me would never have known how much that jump really meant to me. It was not just jumping off a bridge. It had a bigger meaning for me. It meant to let go of the past, move on and to be stronger, but mostly, to believe in myself.

Afterwards, I was filled with adrenaline. I was incredibly proud of myself. What happened at the bungee jump really changed my life completely. While waiting to go out onto the bridge, I saw somebody. A man with dark brown eyes, dark hair with a nicely shaved beard, buff shoulders and a huge tattoo on his back, staring right at me, making me all nervous. I remember thinking this man was the best-looking human I have ever laid my eyes on.

What I did not know back then was this human was about to change my life, forever. The date was December 19th, 2014, and it was the birthday of my dead father.

At that very moment, I did not say hi to the beautiful man. I just secretly looked at him. I tried to impress him by talking loudly and trying to get his attention. When it was finally my turn to get out onto the bridge, I regretted not talking to him, but I would for sure talk to him when I came back from the jump.

To my disappointment, he was gone when I came back.

Two days later, I was out with a couple of friends. While we were walking around in the city, we were all hungry and I pointed at a random restaurant. "Let's go in there, I am starving."

While I was ordering a drink, I could see a group a people walking past me. To my surprise, it was him, the beautiful dark eyed man I had seen two days earlier. I turned around and we made eye contact, but he kept walking right past me out of the restaurant. I kept staring at him, while he was on the other side of the road looking back into the restaurant, staring right back at me. He turned around and came back into the restaurant. I walked towards him. We shook hands and he kissed my hand as he introduced himself – My name is Hector and I am from Uruguay.

"My name is Isabell from Sweden. I saw you at the bungee jump the other day, right?"

"Yes, that was me.

"Where are you going now?" I asked.

"I am going back to Goma, in Congo. I work as a UN military and my bus leaves right now. But if I would have stayed, you would have been my mission."

I blushed. All I could think about was I wanted him to stay.

"I will find you on Facebook, just tell me your whole name."

"Isabell Andersson with two ss. Isabell just like here." I pointed to my foot where I have my name tattooed on my left foot.

Then, he left. I was waiting for him to contact me on Facebook. On Christmas Eve, December 24th, 2014, he wrote to me. This is how we started to build our friendship. We talked through Facebook, writing messages every day. I was telling him about the cities I visited, my adventures and about everything I did on my travels. He told me about life in the Congo.

After a while, we started to send voice messages, which turned into real calls through Facebook Messenger. I remember exactly where I was when I called him the first time. I was in the Philippines in El Nido. I was a little tipsy and finally had the courage to call him. We talked for forty-five minutes until my shitty Wi-Fi died. After that call, we started to call each other every day. When I finally returned to Sweden, we were inseparable. We talked for hours each day. We even slept together on the phone. I called him every night before falling asleep, then we had each other on the line while we fell asleep.

Everything we did was through Wi-Fi; thank god for that invention. On September 15th, 2015, he arrived in Stockholm, Sweden, to finally meet me. It was exactly how I had imagined it would be. Just like in those silly love movies. Everything from the first kiss to our first real date was perfect. When the time came for him to leave after two weeks of spending every second together, I fell apart. It took three months until I saw him again. This is how our journey looked like. Miles apart for months, talking on the phone, sending pictures and writing every day. At one time, we spent five months without seeing each other. On December 19th, 2017, we got married. On the day we first met, but 3 years later.

Hector has given me so many things, but the best thing is he really showed me real love does exists. He made me believe in something I thought did not exist for many years. From being the insecure girl who always said loudly, I will never get married, never will I be with one man for the rest of my life, never will I be cooking for anybody but myself. I am always going to be an independent woman. I am always going to be strong by myself.

Today, I know I was just scared. You can be completely independent while cooking for the one you love and still be a strong human and love yourself.

The hardest thing here was in the beginning of our chapter. I did not love myself at all. The time before meeting Hector, I had so much self-doubt and hate. Thanks to Hector, I learned how to appreciate and love myself. Asking for help does not mean one is weak. It is a sign of courage. Being independent does not mean you have to be all by yourself and do it on your own. Being alone is a weakness. We were meant to always survive in groups together ever since the very beginning of our time.

I isolated myself for years, which made me the girl who thought she did not need anybody. The truth is, I did not need anybody, but I was strong enough to survive and be happy with somebody also. Instead, isolating myself made me feel lonely. I had a hard time getting everything to work between Hector and me because I had that type of mindset for a while. I wanted to do everything by myself. I did not want to show weakness or feelings.

I was a tough cookie to break, but when I finally did break and came out of my shell, it started to be easier between us and finally, we were in symphony. I am so thankful today, that he did not give up on me, especially for all those times I turned around and almost broke up with him because I was scared.

Scared of being left by him, or of him cheating on me. For me, it was easier to leave him first. Instead, I hurt him many times. However, he was always there with open arms, when I broke down and crawled back to him. He understood, and instead of being mad or telling me I was wrong, he pushed me to become better, stronger and loved me even harder at my worst, just as I needed.

True love is not always perfect and pretty. It is simply two imperfect humans coming together and making it work through whatever is thrown at them, together as a team. Instead of seeing each other as enemies, we saw the real in each other, and we became a team that backed up each other, no matter what. Today, he is my best friend, lover and business partner. I also want to point out Hector did not do the work for me; I had to do it myself. Starting to believe in love did not come from him, but it helped that he supported me the way he did. I was the one taking baby steps, trying, fighting and finally letting go of my fears. It is a process and for me, it took so many tries to finally figure it out.

You know if you ever have a thought like, "Oh what the hell, I am better on my own," that is your inner voice trying to convince you about the easy way out.

If the person is treating you wrong, that voice is totally right, and you should listen to it and get out. However, if the person you are with is kind, having patience and trying to love you, but you are in a bad state, then taking the easy way out is the stupidest thing you could do. Love is for me a job, a 24/7 job which never ends. What you put in, is what you get out. If I have a hard day, and I am having an attitude, he takes it. Just the way, I take it when he has his bad days. No point in making it worse. If both of us have a bad day, we give each other more space' but we never try to make it worse for one another.

Life is a big roller coaster. It is hard enough, so trying to make it better and easier for each other is a must in our relationship. There is a rule about give and take. Some days I take 80%, and he only takes 20% and vice versa. It is never really 50/50. I used to believe that is how love was, so anytime it got hard, I wanted to quit. I never really had the patience or the knowledge to know things will work out, and it is not the end of the world after all. Having a past filled with abuse in so many ways, it was super hard for me to get our relationship to work. I had to work on so many areas of myself to get to the point of letting myself trust him. Being in this situation is hard for anybody letting go of their fears, but it is possible and when you do, it can be very beautiful.

Aw i hope your day is going better and easyer, this wifi os sooo sooo slow so i cant even hear the voicemessage 😊 Today we been to the coca canyon and we all are hungover ! It is funny, i think the first time i was to much in my own world, bit its crazy how we meet again, im glad u came back in that restutant 😊

den 26 februari 2015 ·

 Isabell Rodriguez

den 26 februari 2015 ·

 Isabell Rodriguez
Thats for u
den 26 februari 2015 ·

 Héctor Rodriguez Curbelo
Awww
den 26 februari 2015 · Skickat från Messenger

 Héctor Rodriguez Curbelo
You are becoming something I want more and more every day.
Sweetest girl with the sweetest voice ever.
And you are also super sexy. Which helps 😊
den 26 februari 2015 · Skickat från Messenger

Hector Rodriguez Curbelo
I really like us making each others company the way we do.
den 18 mars 2015 · Skickat från Messenger

Isabell Rodriguez
Hahah me to, were awesome ☺
den 18 mars 2015 ·

Héctor Rodríguez Curbelo
Haha yes.
List of things we share:
den 18 mars 2015 · Skickat från Messenger

Héctor Rodríguez Curbelo
1. We both like traveling.
2. We both like doing crazy stuff.
3. We r awesome.
4. U r really sexy and good looking and me... well at least I'm not ugly ☺
5. We both like each other.
6. We both send each other drunk messages.
7. We want to sleep cuddling together.
8. We r from different countries and continents and we met at a third one.
9. We r awesome again.
☺
den 18 mars 2015 · Skickat från Messenger

Isabell Rodriguez
Awwww thats like the cutest ever, hahha and your so right, love that ☺
i will send you a drunk message tonight cuz were going out, hahha told u ☺
den 18 mars 2015 ·

Isabell Rodriguez

den 28 februari 2015 ·

 Héctor Rodríguez Curbelo
You, little girl, have no idea how much I like you... ☺
den 1 mars 2015 · Skickat via nätet

Visa nyare meddelanden...

den 19 mars 2015 · Skickat från Messenger

Héctor Rodríguez Curbelo
Here I am... at my UN truck at the airport... today I had and still have lots to do.
den 19 mars 2015 · Skickat från Messenger

Isabell Rodriguez
You look soo good 😃 wish i could be there with u!! Today we will take another overnight train so packing and getting everything ready 😃
den 19 mars 2015 ·

Héctor Rodríguez Curbelo
I just f*ING love being in touch with u
den 19 mars 2015 · Skickat från Messenger

Visa nyare meddelanden...

Hector Rodriguez Curbelo
Poor you. You really sounded wasted. Take a good rest pretty face
I won't go anywhere. Kiss.

PS: ur in my mind also.

den 10 mars 2015 · Skickat från Messenger

Héctor Rodríguez Curbelo
PS: ur in my mind also.

den 10 mars 2015 · Skickat från Messenger

Isabell Rodriguez

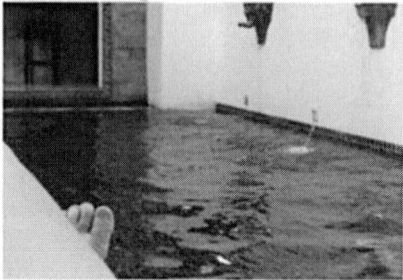

den 10 mars 2015 ·

Isabell Rodriguez
Now im back but soon i will go for the sunset on 4wheels, that will be fun ☺

den 10 mars 2015 ·

Héctor Rodríguez Curbelo
Awwwwww look at that little toe

den 10 mars 2015 · Skickat från Messenger

Isabell Rodriguez

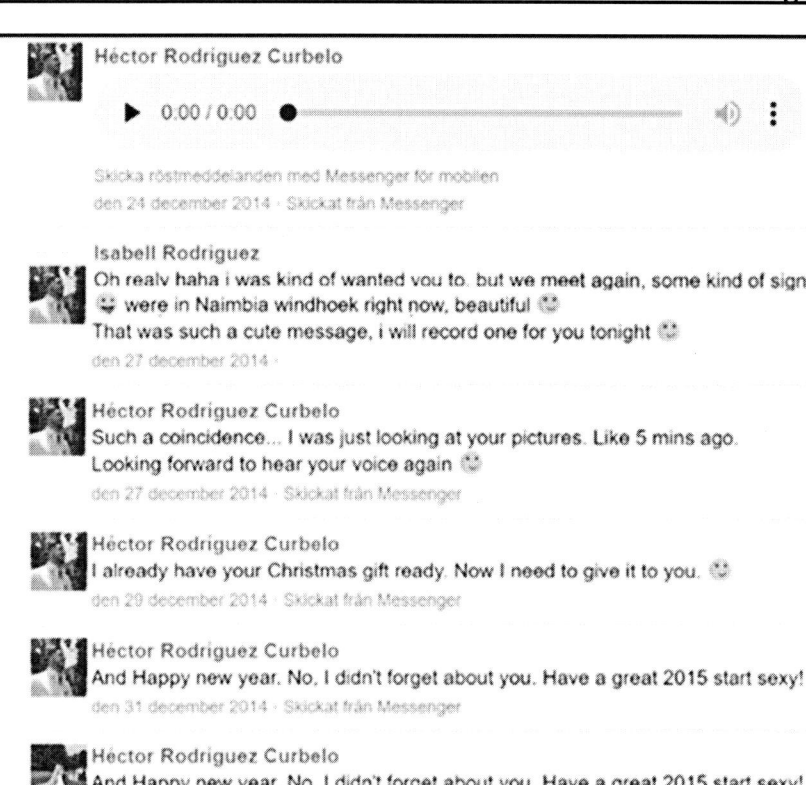

Héctor Rodriguez Curbelo

▶ 0:00 / 0:00 ●━━━━━━━━━━━━━ ◀) ⋮

Skicka röstmeddelanden med Messenger för mobilen
den 24 december 2014 · Skickat från Messenger

Isabell Rodriguez
Oh realy haha i was kind of wanted vou to. but we meet again, some kind of sign ☺ were in Naimbia windhoek right now, beautiful ☺
That was such a cute message, i will record one for you tonight ☺
den 27 december 2014 ·

Héctor Rodriguez Curbelo
Such a coincidence... I was just looking at your pictures. Like 5 mins ago.
Looking forward to hear your voice again ☺
den 27 december 2014 · Skickat från Messenger

Héctor Rodriguez Curbelo
I already have your Christmas gift ready. Now I need to give it to you. ☺
den 29 december 2014 · Skickat från Messenger

Héctor Rodriguez Curbelo
And Happy new year. No, I didn't forget about you. Have a great 2015 start sexy!
den 31 december 2014 · Skickat från Messenger

Héctor Rodriguez Curbelo
And Happy new year. No, I didn't forget about you. Have a great 2015 start sexy!
den 31 december 2014 · Skickat från Messenger

Isabell Rodriguez
HAPPY NEW YEAR ☺ your so cute. i got u something aswell. we need to see eachother again ☺ I am so sorry i forgot to record that message and i havnt have wifi for some days now. hope u

Héctor Rodríguez Curbelo
I just love that little voice of yours
den 7 mars 2015 · Skickat från Messenger

Héctor Rodríguez Curbelo
I was wondering... are you married or engaged or do you have a boyfriend or something?
den 7 mars 2015 · Skickat från Messenger

Héctor Rodríguez Curbelo
I was wondering... are you married or engaged or do you have a boyfriend or something?
It won't change the fact I like you a lot but still 😊
den 7 mars 2015 · Skickat från Messenger

Isabell Rodriguez
Hahah what !? No why would u think that 😊?
I wouldnt be talking to strangers then, your so cute 😊
den 7 mars 2015 ·

Héctor Rodríguez Curbelo
😊
den 7 mars 2015 · Skickat från Messenger

Héctor Rodríguez Curbelo

▶ 0:11 / 0:11 ━━━━━━━━━━━━━━━━━━━━━━━━━━● 🔊 ⋮

Skicka röstmeddelanden med Messenger för mobilen

98

CHAPTER VII:

Turn Your Pain Into Positive Growth

Getting the psychosis was probably the worst, but also the best thing that could have happened to me. I had to deal with certain issues, even though it took me years to recover from it. I went on a journey that made me who I am today and where I am today is far from what I had imagined ten years ago, but that is how it all started.

Even if it was my worst breaking point and I thought I had lost the most important thing in my life, "my mind", I had to work with what I had. I got to know myself in a way I never would have if I did not become psychotic. It was the hardest moment of my life. I thought at times I had gone crazy. I was super scared of being alone with myself. I had a paranoia and an anxiety, which at times, I thought would kill me, literally. My anxiety became so bad I had a fear of being in public.

A few times I vomited because of all the nervousness I felt. The panic attacks made me feel like I was going to either faint or have a heart attack. Anxiety is not dangerous. It will never kill you, even if it sometimes feels like it will, you will not die. These three things have helped me after years of living with constant panic attacks:

1. Write down how you feel when you have anxiety or a panic attack. Everything from your heart beating, your body shaking, to feeling like fainting or losing your breath. Have it near you all the time and read it when you feel like you are about to have one of those episodes. It will help to remind you it is not

dangerous, and you will not die this time either. It also helps to understand and reflect over the symptoms you have. You have felt it before, and you will survive. It will be over soon.

2. I used to breathe in and out while looking at a square, like a window, for example. Breathe in while you concentrate on the top line, then breathe out while concentrate on the right line and so on. This should get your breathing controlled and slow it down to a phase that will calm you down. While I did this, I used to count, 1 2 3... in my head.

3. Listen to a happy song or put on a funny movie (I always found the *Sex and the City* series most helpful) or go for a walk or even a run.

It can always be helpful to call a friend or someone you trust and feel secure with. Sometimes I used to put on high music with earphones and dance hysterically. If you are alone, you can sing out loud. I have done all of these examples, and one of them has always helped me in those moments.

At times, the anxiety can be strong and hard to control. When this happens, I have found that just sitting down, letting it come all over me as a storm, letting it take its place, while not doing anything, has managed to help the panic attack to stop. By doing this, I showed myself it came; it made chaos and then, it disappeared without me dying or anything bad happening, and I got through it.

No pill, or drug or doctor can fix your pain if you are not willing to look inside for the real issue, problem or behavior. Get the knowledge you need to rebuild your life, your behavior and the way you react. It was not my feelings that were my biggest problem. It was my reaction towards them which got me into difficult situations. For many years, I thought I was broken; needing to be fixed. All I really needed was to understand I was not broken; I just needed to find the tools to heal myself.

It took me many sessions of therapy, coaching, self-learning and growth books to get me where I am today. The only thing I really had was the "will" not to accept my life was going to be miserable forever. I knew there was another way out, but I also knew it would take time; years of fighting, hundreds of tries and falling back down. Also, I had to understand life is not perfect, nor is it something called lucky.

Perfect is defined by many people. One person's perfection could be another one's flaws and so on. Lucky is not something you are. Luck is something you create. The more you work towards what you want, the "luckier" you get.

I do believe in the laws of attraction. "The Secret" is both a book and a movie I highly recommend.

Happiness is a state of mind; something that comes and go.

No one is happy 24/7, 365 days a year. Life is all about ups and downs. Unexpected things will happen and you cannot control it, but trying to stay positive helps you move forward, no matter what is going on.

I felt shame, loneliness and anger for so many years because of everything I went through. Terrified to be judged or looked down upon. I was super insecure and even if I never wanted it to show, it was pretty obvious I was. The way I dressed, the way I tried to look perfect, almost as if it was my outside that was the problem, but it was my soul which needed surgery; not my breast, not my face nor anything else for that matter.

By distracting myself from the real problem, I was creating new ones in my head, which really had me doubting myself. Who was I? Why did I feel like I had to be perfect? Why did I have to be the girl everyone wanted to hang out with? I put my standards so up high, I could never live up to them.

I know for sure I am not the only woman, or human for that matter, that has ever felt like this and this is a serious problem. I created the worst enemy inside of myself. I had to kill it. Days still come when I hear the evil voice in my head, but today I know how to handle it.

I will never let my inner saboteur (as I call it) ruin anything for me today. I have come too far to give into the stupid, evil little voice.

I think having a goal when you are in your darkest periods helps. No matter how small or big, it is very important to have at least one goal. For many years, "happy" was my goal, which was impossible. How do you define happy? You cannot be happy all the time. How do you know you are happy? It was too abstract. I had to let that idea go and find another goal. Having a goal as being happy never gave me anything to really reach for. It only gave me negative thoughts like "I just want to be happy. Why can I not just be happy?"

So, instead of trying to reach "happy." I changed it to "find a balance." Not eating too little, not eating too much. Not working too much, not working at all and so on. Finding my gray zone became my goal. I was always a black or white type of person, but I now wanted to be in-between, as much as I could.

It has been a long journey to find the middle, to find my balance. It all started with small baby steps. Many slips and falls, and even more getting up on my feet again. I wish back in the day; I had a book telling me what to do, how to get it done and how to get "strong." However, the truth is, no matter what advice or strategies you get, in the end you need to put them into action and find your own way.

I have tried things for years that studies showed have worked for most people, but they did not work for me. I found other tools and strategies which work specifically just for me. Then, I made up roads as I was going. Today, I am all for learning and discovering new ways of thinking. I am fascinated about how the brain works and how we can work with it to change both behaviors and thoughts. It is also beautiful how you can change and build the life you want, no matter where you come from and whatever struggles you have faced. You always have the option to change it, one way or another, one step at a time.

CHAPTER VIII:

Stepping Out of Your Comfort Zone

I had to get out of my comfort zone many times. It is a state where you are actually scared and free at the same time. Leaving so many times for the unknown became my thing. I ran away to go live in another country, or I went on a world trip. Coming back was the hardest thing for me. Being away was my comfort zone. Going back to the place where I was born, where I had gone through my darkest periods, made me super anxious. I finally came to the moment when I had to move back and stay to really overcome the anxious feelings. I dealt with the fear and worked my way through it, piece by piece.

Thinking I was bipolar for many years, I was taking medication that was not good for my body. I had taken the medication for seven years. It made me doubt if I was able to live a life without it. It left me afraid to have a child because I knew bipolar disorder was genetic. The slightest chance that my baby could get this horrible disorde" was making me doubt having a child at all. I could never live with myself if I knew I was the reason my child was bipolar and had to go through the emotional ride I went through.

Today I know the reason why I had such an emotional ride was because of my earlier traumas. My father died in my early childhood. I was molested when I was four years old. For years, not only did I watch my stepfather abusing my mom, but he also abused me and so did my first boyfriend. Then, I tried to hide all of it by doing drugs, drinking and throwing my life out the door.

Looking back, I realize this was the loneliest road I could possibly go down.

When I started to change my life, doing everything in my power to overcome my depression, my anxieties and my insecurities, I started to see results. I actually felt better and more balanced, but I started to doubt my success because of the medication. What if I feel okay because of the medication? What happens if I stop taking it?

I decided I wanted to stop taking the medication. I wanted to know who I was "today" without it. It took me one year and a half to slowly cut down until I finally stopped taking it. That was a horrible experience. At times I could not sleep and I became super depressed, but the longer I went without the medication, the better and more balanced I became. I finally knew who I would become and how I reacted to "real life" without a substitute that was supposed to keep me "balanced and numb." I knew I had done the real work, not the medication. I could finally see clearly. There was no longer a filter between my emotions and me. Slowly, I accepted myself, my flaws, my past and that is something I keep doing every day. In the back of my mind, I knew it was not because of a medication, not because of love, but because of my hard work that I had overcome my depressions and anxiety.

Quitting alcohol completely, was also a choice I made two and a half years ago. Knowing alcohol brought out the worst side of me, not always, but sometimes; it was not worth it for me anymore. To risk the drunk-side of Isabell to come out and destroy the life I have created was not going to be an option. So, I quit drinking.

I know today I deserve to be living a successful life with love and to be smiling most of the time, but I did not know this six years ago. I had to sacrifice things I thought I could not live without, like alcohol. I have other things in life to fulfill me instead. Like meditation, which is something I do for myself, every morning I meditate, to start my day in peace.

I have a healthier relationship to fitness now and I make sure I recharge my body with healthy food. I love heavy lifting. I combine it with cross-training and long walks. Training for me is so much more than just healthy living; it is also to release emotions and to recharge my "batteries." I had to work on my anger a lot. For many years, I was angry towards men. Considering where I came from, maybe it was not so weird after all. But of course, it was something I had to work on.

It is my responsibility to work on myself. Blaming my past is one of the worst things to do. To take responsibility for me, I had to learn to let go of the hate that a few men had created in my life. I had to stop blaming all men for what these few men had done to me. Not everyone is the same and thinking this way will only hurt you in the end. Dragging everyone over the same line is more hurtful to yourself than to anyone else.

Living in anger will cause you pain. It is not worth it. Get to the root of the problem, admit it, work with it, let it go and move on. It sounds easier than it is, but it can be done. I received help from an amazing coach and therapist and with a lot of hard work on my end to remove the hate I had built up deep inside of me for years.

Today, I am an international speaker, author and a mental health coach. To know more about my journey, visit my blog at www.issyrodriguez.com, where I share my experience, ideas and my daily life. If you want me to help you personally, join me on my next workshop, where we will go through your story together and I will help you unlock the best version of yourself. To know more about the "Rebuild Your Life" program and workshop, go to www.rebuildyourlifeprogram.com I have chosen to share my story to help others in every way I can. I want to inspire others and reach people who are in situations like the one I once was in, so they will feel less lonely and hopeless, because I know how hard it can be at times.

I want people to understand that no matter what journey you are on, whatever you have been through, how old you are, or whatever you want to do in life, you can change your present and become the best version of yourself. If I can change my life, you can too.

Never let your past decide where you are going with your future. I know who I am today is the person I needed to talk to ten years ago. Learning is a process which never ends; which is amazing. If you think about it, the older you get, the more you know and the more you can teach and give back to the world.

CHAPTER IX:
Say Something

The documentary my mom and I decided to be a part of actually became bigger than we could ever have imagined. It started with us wanting to tell our story to becoming something much bigger. I also felt I received so much from it; it was like a therapy. It helped my mom and I to get closer. It opened up a new world because of all the people who watched it as well.

Many people reached out to me and thanked me for sharing my story, for being so woundable and open, and for telling my truth. It meant so much for me that they actually took their time to write to me. It made me feel proud that somehow sharing my pain helped others to feel less alone. My story showed them somebody they could relate to which hopefully gave them the strength to keep fighting.

While they were filming our lives for five years, I changed and so did my relationship with my mother. Our relationship was destroyed when we left Ben and it became even worse throughout my teenage years. I could not handle it when my mom tried to regain the parenting role, she basically had lost because of him and his abuse which mentally degraded her.

I handled my experience by doing everything a parent does not want their kids to do. I was a nightmare for my mom, even if I never meant to put her through that nightmare. It was just how I dealt with everything. I remember my mom begging me to get help, especially when I was sick with anorexia. She was crying. When I got depressed, she would sit by my bed while I was sleeping all day long. The only time I got up was when I went to the bathroom.

At one time, she called the ambulance because I had not left the bed for over a week. But whatever I went through, that woman would never leave my side and she never stopped fighting for me, which is something I am forever grateful for. I think my mom was a superhero-mother at times.

Yes, she could have done things differently, but we all could do things in a better way. We are humans and we are not born with all the answers or with a map of our life in our hands. We learn as we grow. Some people even blamed her after seeing the documentary. They were blaming her for what I had been through, but I do not agree with them at all.

My mother never wanted to meet a psychopath. She was attracted to the wrong men because of her own traumas and how it shaped her into believing she did not deserve more. But it was never her fault it turned out the way it did for me. She did the best she could in every situation for me and my brother, always, but I know she blames herself, even today.

Today, I thank her. Because of what I went through with my experiences, I am a strong woman. I thank her for being a strong woman who never gave up, which also reflected on me, because throughout my darkest moments, I never gave up. Everything can be analyzed or seen either in a positive way or a negative way. If you are negative, you get problems, dramas and misery. But on the other hand, if you choose to see the positive and are analyzing things from an optimistic point of view, then it is easier to find the solutions and the answers you are looking for. Why? Because a negative person always focuses on the problem and a positive person focuses on the opportunities that come when you solve the problems. There is always a solution; you just need to find it.

The "Say Something" documentary gave us more room to rebuild our relationship and we became closer because of it. We went to interviews and shared stages together. We even went into the Swedish government office to tell our story; how the system did not work, how the women's shelter can improve and what our experience was.

Things are now changing and a new law in Sweden against children who witness violence at home is being submitted. We were able to tell our story from the child and the mother's point of view. Not only did the documentary help others, but hopefully it will have an impact on the law.

2017 was a big year for us when we were nominated at the Swedish "Kristallen gala" for the best documentary. I remember being so nervous. It was a great experience for both of us. When they announced we had won, we both just lost it. It was unreal and going up on the stage was a crazy feeling, but we were so proud. Happy to be sharing that moment together. We were no longer victims; we were warriors who had survived to help others in similar situations. We were so honored to have won the prize.

I will never forget that moment. It is something my mom and I will always share together. I believe anyone can change their future; change their life, their behavior and the way they think. I am far from where I want to be, but I have come a long way.

The most important message I want you as a reader to keep with you after reading this book is**: no matter how hard your life is or how low you might be, there is always a way out.**

Maybe you know somebody or you will meet someone who cannot seem to keep their head above the water. Loneliness is a tough feeling, but just by being there, supporting them, you can help them feel less abandoned. You are never alone, and although it can feel like you are, the more you open up and "say something", the less lonely you will be.

For me, my journey has become a tool to help others. If I can manage to change at least one life, then I know my story was not for nothing.

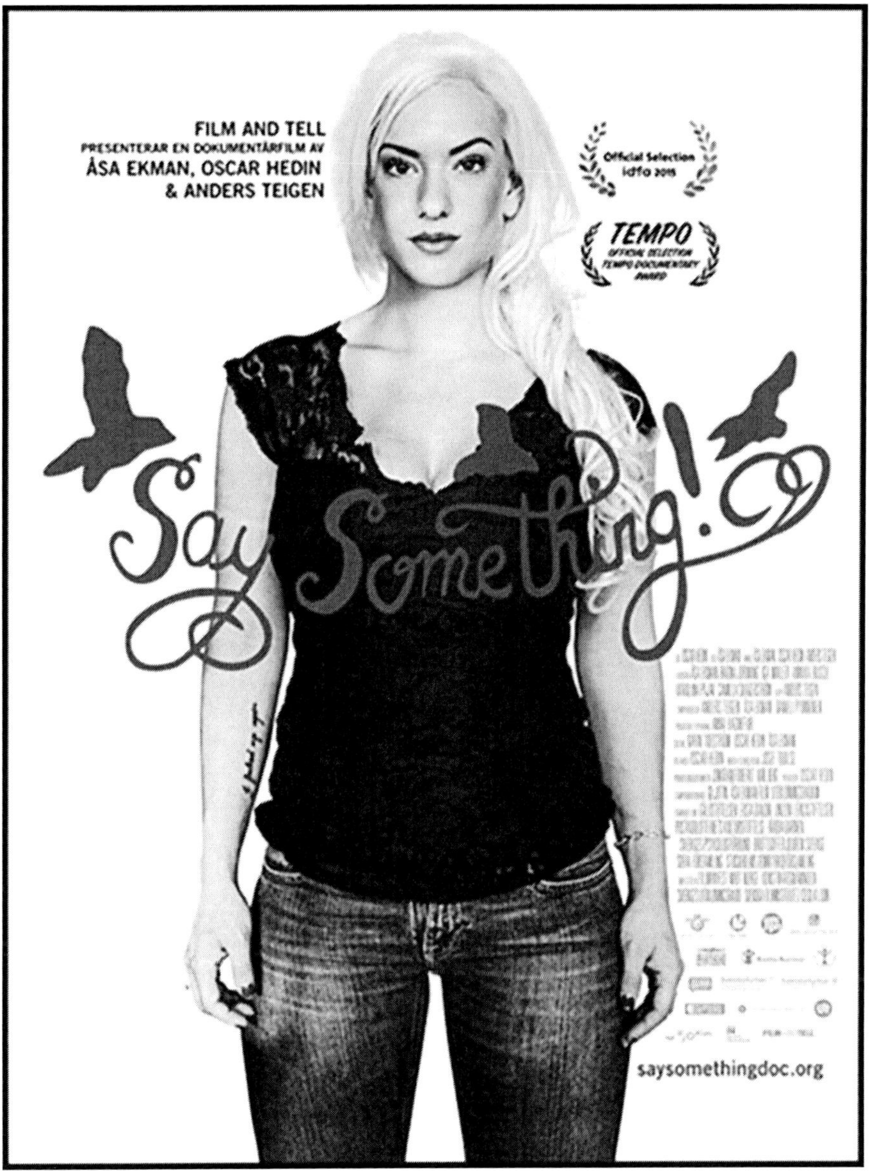

KRISTALLEN
DET SVENSKA TEVEPRISET

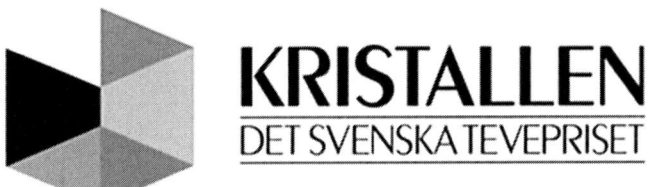